ENIGMA:
THE UNTOLD STORY OF THE SECRET CAPTURE

ENIGMA:
THE UNTOLD STORY OF THE SECRET CAPTURE

VOLUME 3 OF *THE BRITISH NAVY AT WAR AND PEACE*

DAVID BALME

SERIES EDITOR: CAPTAIN PETER HORE

Whittles Publishing

Published by
Whittles Publishing Ltd.,
Dunbeath,
Caithness, KW6 6EG,
Scotland, UK

www.whittlespublishing.com

Series editor: Captain P. G. Hore FRHistS CMIL RN rtd

Volume 1: *Wingfield at War*
ISBN 978-184995-064-0

Volume 2: *Through Albert's Eyes*
ISBN 978-184995-066-4

ISBN 978-184995-226-2

Printed by Gomer Press

CONTENTS

Foreword
Series Editor's Foreword
1 Midshipman David Balme
2 The Loss of HMS *Courageous*
3 The Sinking of *U-42* and *U-45*
4 Sub Lieutenants' Courses, Portsmouth
5 The Battle of Cape Spartivento
6 The Fight with the Heavy Cruiser *Hipper*
7 HMS *Bulldog*
8 The Battle for Convoy OB318
9 The Death of Fritz-Julius Lemp
10 The Ransack of *U-110*
11 The Prize from *U-110*
12 Untold Gold
13 The Cloak of Secrecy
14 Operation Harpoon
15 Operations over the Western Desert
16 Fighter Direction Officer
17 Churchill's Private Yacht
18 War against Japan
19 Home Again
20 The Hollywood Years
21 Coda
Appendix A – Abstract of the Signals Log
Appendix B – The Timetable of Operation Primrose
Bibliography
Notes

David Balme (1920–2016)

FOREWORD

In three short years, between 1972 and 1974, two great secrets of the Second World War were disclosed to an astonished public. In *The Double Cross System in the War of 1939 to 1945*, Sir John Masterman explained how the network of Nazi spies in Britain had been entirely controlled by the Security Service, MI5. Encouraged by this precedent, Frederick Winterbotham revealed, in *The Ultra Secret*, the huge code breaking operation at Bletchley Park that had given Allied strategists vital access to Nazi communications at key moments in the conflict. Both disclosures set the scene for Professor R.V. Jones's classic memoir *Most Secret War*, which, in 1978, laid out the whole panorama of scientific warfare in fascinating detail.

In a US bookstore in the early 1990s, I discovered an aspect of the story that took me by surprise: the supposedly unbreakable codes had been cracked by more than just intellectual effort. *Seizing the Enigma*, by David Kahn, gave a gripping account of efforts to achieve 'short cuts' – by capturing enemy warships before their coding machines, adjustable rotors or lists of settings could all be destroyed. Central to the narrative was the boarding of *U-110* by David Balme, a very junior naval officer, just out of his teens, and a handful of brave seamen who had rowed to the submarine in a tiny open boat.

This history-changing encounter very nearly did not happen: the escort force commander was about to order the ramming of *U-110* when a distant memory flashed into his mind. It was of a Staff College lecture on the capture of the German cruiser *Magdeburg* by the Russians in the First World War, and the treasure trove of cipher material handed to the Admiralty as a result. Thus did a vital lesson from an earlier conflict lead to decisive success in a later one – a point particularly appealing to me as a military historian.

The constituency of New Forest East was created, as a result of boundary changes, in the run-up to the 1997 General Election. Having been selected the previous year as prospective parliamentary candidate, I was invited to meet local Party activists at the home of Joan Nabarro, the widow of a famous and colourful Conservative MP. In conversation she mentioned that her brother-in-law, David Balme, was also a local supporter and asked if I had met him. "No," I replied, but I recognised the name and added, "but was he in the Royal Navy in the Second World War?" She confirmed that he was. "In that case, he was responsible for one of the greatest intelligence coups of the Battle of the Atlantic!"

And so I became a friend of this delightful and courageous man whose perilous mission, and its consequences, had been too little known for half a century. As Peter Hore describes, in his chapter 'The Hollywood Years', it eventually proved possible – to some extent – to make amends. Now, this stirring biography should ensure a permanent place for David Balme in the roster of quiet heroes on whom a country like ours depends.

Rt Hon Dr Julian Lewis MP

SERIES EDITOR'S FOREWORD

David Balme will be forever known as the man who, as a twenty-year old sub lieutenant, boarded and ransacked a German U-boat in mid-Atlantic, thereby capturing one of the greatest secrets of the Second World War, a capture – or 'pinch' as it was known in inner circles – that changed the course of the Battle of the Atlantic and shortened the war itself.

Of course, Balme acted as part of a team, a team made up of the officers and men of the 3rd Escort Group so ably led by Commander Joe Baker-Cresswell, and part of the time at least Balme shared the danger with other unsung heroes, including Lieutenant Commander George Dodds. Yet Balme's bravery was exceptional. No red mist of anger fell upon him driving him to impetuous action: rather he had some time to confront his fears and to contemplate the many ways of dying when exposed in the ocean in HMS *Bulldog*'s whaler, while boarding *U-110* and when conducting, alone, the first search of the U-boat. He risked being shot, blown up or drowned, and when *Bulldog* disappeared into the Atlantic mist to hunt another U-boat, he risked being sunk. Yet where others tried and failed, or tried and tragically lost their lives, Balme and the boarding party succeeded magnificently in capturing Enigma and associated cipher material.

The capture was so secret that few on the British side knew about it and not even the Americans were told, after they entered the war, what had been achieved. When Captain S.W. Roskill wrote the official history, *The War at Sea*, he was not told of it despite the access he was given to other secret records, and when in 1959 he wrote *The Secret Capture*, he was forbidden by the authorities from mentioning the true nature of the secret.

Meanwhile, the hero, David Balme, returned to marry his beautiful Susan, and never spoke about the capture, knowledge of which, he thought, would be buried forever. He even obeyed a restriction on his overseas travel, at the expense of his legitimate post-war business as a wool broker. However, when the wider secret of Bletchley was revealed and others began to write about it, Balme made several essays at writing his story, he corresponded with some of the participants in his story, and late in life he made several recordings.

As the reader will learn, besides the capture of *U-110*, Balme also enjoyed an astonishing variety of experience, which covered the Spanish Civil War, the Palestine Patrol, the sinking of HMS *Courageous*, the Battle of Convoy KJF3, the fight with the heavy cruiser *Hipper*, the Battle of Cape Spartivento, the Battle of Convoy OB318, Operation Harpoon, the air war in the Western Desert, the high level diplomacy of Prime Minister Winston Churchill, and pioneering work as a fighter direction officer in the war against Japan. David Balme's accounts inevitably overlap and repeat, and *Enigma: The Untold Story of the Secret Capture* is a synthesis of his own stories about his war, and its aftermath.

When I interviewed David Balme in 2000 for an op-ed piece I was writing for *Newsday* in New York I had little idea that I would have the privilege of editing these memoirs. For assistance in this work I am grateful to many people including Susan Dearing, Malcolm Dodds, Jock Gardner, David Hobbs, Julian Lewis, Jonathan Mostow, Ninian Stewart, John de Winton and Richard Woodman, and I am especially grateful to Susan Balme for allowing me access to David's papers.

Peter Hore

1

MIDSHIPMAN DAVID BALME

"This is David Balme and I'm going to try to record the various actions I was in during the war."[1]

So start David Balme's spoken memoirs. In the beginning of the Second World War 18-year old Balme was still an officer under training, a midshipman in the destroyer HMS *Ivanhoe*.

David Edward Balme, whose family traced their Huguenot ancestry back to Henri IV's France, was born in Kensington on 1 October 1920, the second son of a family of five children, and spent his childhood in Wimbledon and later at Doone House prep in Sussex. Family lore holds that the Balmes originated in Savoy in the tenth century. The family once lived in the cave complex at Balme les Grottes, east of Lyon, and later in La Rochelle allied themselves to Henri of Navarre and married into the French royal family. The Balme family were in Paris for Henri's marriage to Margaret of Valois when in August 1572 they were swept up the St Bartholomew's Day Massacre of French Protestants by the Catholics, and all were murdered except one boy, François Balme, who was rowed down the Seine by a family retainer and made his escape via Guernsey to England. Many Huguenot refugees had settled in Yorkshire as sheep farmers and there the Balmes took root. By the early nineteenth century they were leaders in the wool brokering business.

When Australia began to export good quality Merino wool to England, the Balmes moved their business to London. Charles Balme set up shop in 1820 in Garraway's coffee house in the City, and they expanded their business overseas. By the start of the twentieth century David's father, Jack Balme, had offices in London and Bradford and handled sales on behalf of suppliers in Australia and South Africa. He was also a member of the Honourable Artillery Company, and he fought and was severely wounded in the face as a territorial in the First World War.

Traditionally in the Balme family the eldest son joined the family firm and the younger sons went to sea. So David's elder brother joined the company in 1928, while young David's interest in the Navy was encouraged by his grandfather, Commander George Hodgkinson, who had served with King George V. He learned to sail during family holidays in Cornwall, the Scilly Islands and the Isle of Wight, and entered the Royal Naval College at Dartmouth in the Anson term of 1934 when he was just aged 13. He did well there, came top in seamanship and gained 4½ months seniority on passing out. Even while still a midshipman his naval career was unusually varied and eventful. In May 1938 he joined the cruiser HMS *London* in the Mediterranean, moving five months later to another cruiser, HMS *Shropshire*, flagship of the 1st Cruiser Squadron.

As has been required of all midshipmen for several centuries, Balme also kept a journal. Balme's opens on 29 May 1938 and the last entry occurs on 17 October 1939. In addition to the professional, mainly seamanship, subjects that Balme's wrote about, he also recorded events during the Spanish Civil War, including an essay, in imitation of Mahan, on 'The Influence of Sea Power on the Spanish War', as well as commenting both on the rising tension throughout Europe and on the lighter side of naval life, from boat work to balls and parties ashore.

It was customary for midshipmen during their sea time to serve both in large ships (cruisers and above) and in smaller ships. So in May 1939 Balme "was suddenly told to pack and be ready to leave for minesweepers" – he was being sent to the fleet minesweeper HMS *Sutton*. *Sutton* had been built in Scotland during the First World War, but she had seen little service and was laid up in reserve at Alexandria, Egypt. She was still in her pre-war livery and with her black hull and light upper works she looked at first glance like a liner, but she was, as Balme wrote, a ship of the 'Black Navy', that is coal-fired and very dirty. *Sutton* was employed on the pre-war Palestine Patrol, on which Balme reflected: "With the increased persecution of the Jews on Germany and now also in Czechoslovakia which is part of Greater Germany, thousands of Jews are being driven out of their homes ... it is a pathetic and incredible state of affairs for the year AD 1939".

Britain held a mandate from the League of Nations over Palestine, whose majority Arab population was being rapidly outnumbered by Jewish refugees from Europe. The Royal Navy's task was not to stop refugees arriving by boat but to keep a look out and to report to the Palestine authorities. An observant young Balme noted the contradiction in the orders given to *Sutton* and to the 3rd Minesweeping Squadron. They had been sent to "to put an end to the landing of illegal immigrants ... but were not allowed to take any action at all to prevent a ship landing, except to warn the master of the penalties". At his young age in *Sutton*, Balme found himself assistant executive officer, accountant officer, captain's secretary and cypher officer – quite a responsibility for an 18-year-old. He was also officer of quarters at *Sutton*'s ancient 4-inch gun, a gun that had not, he wrote, been fired for more than five years. When *Sutton* intercepted *Otrato*, a Panamanian-flagged freighter with 400 Polish Jews embarked, Balme was ordered to fire a warning shot across her bows. There was "an almighty bang and flash. The gun had fired and," he wrote, "everyone was still intact." Faced by this impressive display of firepower, *Otrato* obeyed the order to stop and be searched.

HMS Sutton from Midshipman Balme's journal (Balme)

After six weeks, more modern ships became available for the Palestine Patrol and Balme transferred on 20 June 1939 at Haifa in Palestine to the modern destroyer HMS *Ivanhoe*. She was an I-Class fleet destroyer ordered from Yarrow's at Scotstoun under the 1935 programme. She was oil-fired, steam-driven, armed with four 4.7-inch guns in single mountings, two quintuple torpedo tubes, depth charge racks and throwers, and fitted for – but not with – minesweeping gear. She was capable of 35 knots. But, as far as Balme was concerned, "the most noticeable point was the cleanliness of a modern destroyer in comparison to an old coal-burning minesweeper. Not only upperdeck smartness, but also all fittings and flats below are very clean. The majority of fittings such as ladder rails, are chromium instead of brass [i.e. they did not need to be polished] as in older ships".

HMS Ivanhoe from Midshipman Balme's journal (Balme)

A typical incident on the Palestine Patrol involved *Las Perlas*, a 200-ton schooner flying the flag of Panama. At 21:30 on the evening of Saturday, 1 July, while 30 miles off the coast and well outside territorial waters, *Ivanhoe* saw an SOS flashed by light and the two letter message in international code meaning that a ship had a mutiny aboard and required assistance. This came from *Las Perlas*, but it was ruse intended to have her seized and escorted into Palestine waters under the protection of the Royal Navy. The boarding officers from *Ivanhoe* found that her 370 passengers, who had boarded five days earlier on the Black Sea coast, were indeed menacing the master but this was because he was refusing to take them anywhere but Beirut in French-held Lebanon and not to a port in Palestine for which they had paid. The passengers also claimed to be without food, water or medical supplies, but the boarding officers found no sign of an actual disturbance, and since *Las Perlas* was seaworthy and capable of making port on her own she was allowed to proceed. Reflecting the contradiction in the orders, *Las Perlas*'s master was warned by *Ivanhoe*'s captain, Commander Basil Jones, that if she crossed the 3-mile limit she would be arrested.

At dawn on Sunday morning she was duly found inside territorial waters and when *Ivanhoe*'s officers boarded her, this time they found that the master had been locked in his cabin, and a smouldering fire had broken out in one of the coal bunkers. The passengers had to be roused to help douse the fire with sea water, but farce now turned to tragedy, and while bread, cooked specially in *Ivanhoe*'s galley, was being distributed among the passengers, Able Seaman Robert W. Carr, while leaning over to comfort a woman, who had been overcome by the heat and congestion, accidentally shot himself in the chest. Now the roles changed. A Jewish doctor treated Carr while *Ivanhoe* rushed her casualty into Haifa, and Carr was taken to the British Military Hospital. *Las Perlas* followed *Ivanhoe* into Haifa.[2] Poor Carr died shortly after admission to hospital and his funeral the next day, Monday, was attended by most of the passengers from *Las Perlas*.

The Jewish refugee ship Las Perlas alongside HMS Ivanhoe (Balme)

These difficult and unpleasant duties of the Palestine Patrol continued in a similar vein for two more months, but war clouds were gathering over Europe and Sunday, 3 September found Ivanhoe homebound at high speed across the Mediterranean. Balme wrote in his journal:

> "By the forenoon, we found ourselves close to Crete. It was a glorious day and we were sheltered from the wind by this mountainous island, *Ivanhoe* and *Impulsive* separated from the remainder of the flotilla at 12:00, and we set course for Antikithera Straits which we were going to patrol.
>
> "We had come out of the lee of Crete by now and there was a strong breeze blowing. The sea was a mass of white horses which was a fine sight with the mountains in the background. At 12:30, just as we were changing over watches, the familiar toot-toot came up from the wireless office which means there is a signal to be hauled up through the voice pipe. It was just a meaningless plain language message from the Admiralty with the words "Total Germany" on it – it was the signal [we] had been expecting for some days, Thus Great Britain had issued an ultimatum to Germany, and as no satisfactory answer had been received within two hours, we had declared war."

The Second World War had begun.

2

THE LOSS OF HMS *COURAGEOUS*

By the middle of September 1939 *Ivanhoe* was in Plymouth, where the 3rd Destroyer Flotilla was formally transferred from the Mediterranean Fleet to the Western Approaches Command. The first few weeks of the war were dramatic enough for Balme, who recalled:

> "My birthday is 1st October so just after the war been going a month or so, I was 18 and I was in the destroyer *Ivanhoe*, escorting HMS *Courageous*, I think the actual date was the 20th September 1939 and suddenly, it was about suppertime, there was a big bang in our destroyer and the Maltese steward we had come rushing down the wardroom where we were just having supper and said '*Courageous* has been hit, sinking.'
>
> "So we all dashed up on deck and there the *Courageous* was heeling right over already although it was only a matter of two or three minutes since she was hit by a torpedo from a submarine and she went down very quickly. This was a terrific loss to the British because we only had three big aircraft carriers, the essential ship for any action in naval warfare.
>
> "And so we started picking up the survivors and getting them warm and fed, and putting them down below, and then eventually later on in the evening we headed for Plymouth to take them all back, which was probably 150 miles away. So

that was the first big loss that the British had – headlines in all the papers and a terrific blow to our morale."

The aircraft carrier HMS *Courageous* had been built as a battlecruiser during the First World War when, armed with 15-inch guns, she had taken part in the Second Battle of Heligoland Bight in November 1917. At the end of the war she was also present at the surrender of the German High Seas Fleet in 1918. In the interwar years she was rebuilt as an aircraft carrier, and she was serving in the Home Fleet at the start of the Second World War.

HMS Courageous flying off her Swordfish (Navy photo).

On 3 September 1939 *Courageous* sailed from Plymouth with an escort of destroyers for an anti-submarine patrol in the Western Approaches. Embarked were two naval air squadrons, 811 and 822 NAS, each of twelve Fairey Swordfish torpedo bombers, the famous 'Stringbags'. A fortnight later *Courageous* was off the coast of Ireland, when in the afternoon of 17 September 1939 a wireless signal was received from the British cargo ship SS *Kafiristan* saying that she was under fire from a German U-boat (this was the *U-53*). Two destroyers, HMS *Inglefield* and *Intrepid*, and four aircraft were sent to investigate, and at about 19:30 *Courageous* had turned into wind to recover these aircraft and she had settled on a steady flying course. However, a second U-boat was lurking nearby and Kapitänleutnant Otto Schuhart in *U-29* could scarcely believe his luck: he had been trying to get into a firing position on *Courageous* for some hours and now the carrier presented herself as an ideal target. At 19:50 he fired three torpedoes, two hit the carrier and she immediately listed to port and sank after just seventeen minutes.

While Balme's *Ivanhoe* and *Impulsive* searched for *U-29*, the survivors were rescued by the American freighter *Collingsworth*, the British merchantman *Dido* and the Dutch liner *Veendam*. Other ships, including according to Balme *Ivanhoe*, joined in the search and rescue, but more than 500 men and all the aircraft were lost. The Admiralty quickly realised that its tactic of forming submarine hunting groups around fleet carriers was flawed, and it was abandoned until later in the war when, with more experience, escort carriers became available in large numbers.

While Balme recorded the dismay felt throughout the Royal Navy at the loss of *Courageous*, in Germany the commander of the German submarine force, Befehlshaber der Unterseeboote or BdU, Karl Dönitz, the commander of the German U-boat force, rejoiced and there was widespread jubilation in the Kriegsmarine. Schuhart was awarded the Iron Cross First Class and each one of the crew of *U-29* were awarded the Iron Cross Second Class.

3

THE SINKING OF *U-42* AND *U-45*

Meanwhile, for Balme in *Ivanhoe* there were more convoy duties:

> "So that [the sinking of HMS *Glorious*] was one of the first actions of the war and I was in it.
>
> "And so the rest of that autumn nothing very spectacular happened to me. We were on convoy duties trying to get used to submarine warfare. The U-boats could see a convoy from miles away, because there were so many ships in a convoy, so they could gradually approach it and torpedo various ships probably two at a time.
>
> "Those first few months of the war were terribly strenuous. At sea almost the whole time. [As I said] we could refuel at sea, and on and on we went. It was worst at night, because, of course, we had no lights on, you could hardly see the ship ahead of you, especially in really bad weather, it was very worrying, and you strained your eyes like anything.
>
> "So this routine went on week after week for those first few months of the war while we were trying to get the hang of running the navy on a wartime basis, and I have never felt so tired in my life. I was only 19 then and I needed a lot of sleep and didn't get much."

Konteradmiral Karl Dönitz was to make sure Balm got even less sleep. In October 1939, from his headquarters, which were still in Germany, he had sailed six U-boats in an intended co-ordinated deployment: five boats sailed north about the British Isles, while one boat took a short cut through the English Channel. The later struck a mine and was lost, while the remaining five boats were ordered to rendezvous in the Western Approaches under the tactical command of Korvettenkapitän Werner Hartmann. Hartmann, who would in time become a U-boat ace, was given tactical command of the first wolf packs to be formed during the early stages of the Battle of the Atlantic.[3] The German signals intelligence branch, the B-Dienst, had penetrated British naval codes and was able to detect from its analysis of the wireless (i.e. radio) signal traffic that Convoy KJF3, which had originated in the Caribbean, had been joined by ships from North America, and was nearing the South West Approaches, inbound to the United Kingdom. German U-boat command ordered Hartmann to intercept, but the attack developed over several days in an unco-ordinated free for all. The convoy was also strongly defended by the I-class ships of the 3rd Destroyer Flotilla, and well-led from the destroyer leader *Inglefield*, under Captain Arthur Talbot.

Few U-boat commanders were as unlucky as Fregattenkapitän Rolf Dau on his first patrol in *U-42*, and who had the misfortune to meet the freighter, SS *Stonepool*, belonging to the Sir R. Ropner line, before she reached the rendezvous. *Stonepool* under her master, Albert Smith, was steaming independently south-west of the coast of Ireland, carrying good Welsh coal for St Vincent in the Cape Verde Islands, when at 06:15 on 12 October dawn revealed the tramp ship and the U-boat to each other, on each other's beam and about 3 miles apart. Dau chose to attack by gunfire. However, *Stonepool* was well-skippered, well-organised and she carried a 4-inch stern-chaser, which she manned in about two minutes and began to exchange shot for shot with the enemy. *U-42* hit *Stonepool* but accurate return fire from Smith's ship damaged the German and Dau dived, leaving his gun crew in the water, while *Stonepool* wirelessed the U-boat alarm, 'SSS'. Smith soon saw the German U-boat surface again, apparently for Dau to pick up his gun crew, but unaware that the destroyers *Imogen*, commanded by Commander E. B. K. Stevens, and *Ilex*, commanded by Lieutenant Commander Philip Saumarez, were racing in to the attack. *U-42* dived again but the destroyers fixed the U-boat on the ASDIC underwater detection device, and opened an accurate and brutal attack with depth charges. As *U-42* burst to the surface once more, the destroyers opened fire with their guns. *Ilex* rushed up to ram, but backed off when she realised that the U-boat was doomed and sinking. Sixteen crew survived and were made prisoners of war.[4]

White was awarded the MBE for his "resolute and skilful action ... the discipline was excellent and the gunlayer [ex-RN seaman gunner John Hayter] and the gun's crew [which included 62-year old Steward John Shipman] did very well." This was, the *London Gazette* noted, "the first straight fight in this war between a defensively armed merchantman and a U-boat."

Stonepool, with her stern gun, fought off the U-42 for four hours (Author's collection)

The record books say that this action took place on 13 October, Balme's midshipman's journal says it was in the day before:

> "Friday 12 October ... three weeks at sea with only one full day at Plymouth, but this is a war and work is calling us ... *Inglefield*, *Intrepid*, *Ivanhoe* and later *Icarus*, who had to recall all her men from 48 hours leave. The second wave of U-boats

> had arrived and we after them. Many British merchantships were now armed and one, *Stonepool*, had fought a U-boat for 4 hours. It was *U-42* who was duly sunk by *Imogen*."

Two days later, on the morning of 14 October 1939, three more U-boats of wolf pack Hartmann did find Convoy KJF3 about 230 miles south-west of Fastnet. *U-45 w*as one of these, commanded by Kapitänleutnant Alexander Gelhaar, who had commanded her from new in 1938. Gelhaar's month-long first patrol had been fruitless, but on this, his second patrol, he attacked and reported sinking three big steamers. In fact, he had hit two ships, *Lochavon* and the French *Bretagne*, which were sunk, but a third British steamer, *Karamea*, escaped, apparently because a torpedo detonated prematurely. Retribution was swift: how or why *U-45* was found late the same day is not clear, but she was hunted and depth-charged some 170 nm west of Mizen Head, Ireland, by the British I-destroyers *Icarus*, *Inglefield*, *Intrepid* and *Ivanhoe* and sank with the loss of all thirty-eight of her crew. Balme's version read:

> "Saturday 13 October. At 08:00 we had arrived in the area, and were racing towards a ship which was being chased by a submarine. On sighting her we commenced patrol – *Inglefield* then said they saw the sub which is doubtful. However in the afternoon, all ships gained a contact and numerous attacks were made. *Ivanhoe* made two attacks and we believe the second one was successful as wreckage came to the surface."

Ivanhoe's eventful patrol ended quietly:

> "Sunday 14 October Again today we were racing towards another sinking. This time a French ship, *Vermont*, who was sunk by gunfire – submarines conserving their supplies of torpedoes. At 16:00 we sighted two small boats – these contained 42 survivors, two killed, and *Inglefield* took them aboard. We commenced a search but two ships were not

enough (we had left the other two on yesterday's fighting grounds).

"Monday 15 October. We were 600 miles out in the Atlantic and our fuel was getting short, so we turned towards home."

Two other U-boats of Hartmann's pack did later made contact with the Convoy KJF3, but there was no co-ordinated attack, and Dönitz, who over-estimated the success of his boats and the extent of the British losses, interpreted the attack as validating his ideas about wolf pack tactics. Nevertheless, post-war analysis credited the ships of the 3rd Destroyer Flotilla with two kills in two days, while wolf pack Hartmann overall suffered 50 per cent losses.

Balme had made his last entry in his midshipman's journal and he left *Ivanhoe* at Chatham. Shortly afterwards *Ivanhoe* transferred to the 5th Destroyer Flotilla and on 14 November 1939 she went into refit for the minelaying duties for which her class had been intended.

4

SUB LIEUTENANTS' COURSES, PORTSMOUTH

Large numbers of Royal Naval Volunteer Reserve (RNVR) officers were trained by the Royal Navy in the Second World War and they bore the brunt of the fighting, in ships, submarines, aircraft and every other branch of the Navy. However, although the world was at war and great changes were afoot, the Admiralty had a long-term view and its own continuity and the training of its career officers was uninterrupted, even if some courses were curtailed.

> "Well, that was the first bit of the war for me. Then I went ashore as a sub-lieutenant and did courses in all the subjects

Balme (circled) on his sub lieutenant's course in 1940 (Balme)

> like torpedoes, gunnery, navigation and signals. In the old days that would have taken two years, and we did it all in about four months but got a good smattering of the whole organisation. The courses were shortened and concentrated early on in the war and we spent three or four months doing torpedoes and gunnery and signals."

Under the Molotov–Ribbentrop Pact, Russia and Germany had divided Romania, Poland, Lithuania, Latvia, Estonia, and Finland into spheres of interest, and in November 1939 Russia invaded Finland. The Finns fought back bravely and held up the Soviet army in the Winter War of 1939–40, while Britain and France planned to send 20,000 men to reinforce the Finns. When Denmark, Norway and Sweden declared they would not allow troops to transit their territories en route to Finland, the Finns began to lose heart and started to sue for peace. When the British and French learned of this, the Anglo–French plan was dropped.

> "This was the time when there was a flap on in Finland and we got the Russians and Germans fighting and we put together an expeditionary force of everybody in the army who could ski, and my brother John was in this expeditionary force, and I remember picking him up in our old car and taking him to a ship, I think it was in the east coast, where they were going to sail for Finland. Thank heavens, the Finnish war finished and they never got going because I think they would have been killed – we were such amateurs at doing snow warfare."

5

THE BATTLE OF CAPE SPARTIVENTO

"And then I went to sea in June 1940 in one of our big cruisers, an 8-inch gun cruiser, HMS *Berwick*."

HMS *Berwick* was a heavy cruiser built under the terms of the 1922 Washington Naval Treaty for the defence of the Empire. She was built by the Fairfield Shipbuilding and Engineering Company in Govan, Scotland, launched on 30 March 1926, and first commissioned on 12 July 1927. Built for speed and range, with her three funnels, 10,000 tons standard displacement and 8 × 8-inch guns, *Berwick* was distinctive and impressive. She and her sister ships, *Cornwall*, *Cumberland*, *Kent*, and *Suffolk* and the Australian ships *Australia* and *Canberra*, served successfully in every theatre of the Second World War.

HMS Berwick's three funnels gave her a distinctive silhouette (Balme)

Balme joined *Berwick* on 11 June 1940 in Cammell Laird's shipyard, Birkenhead, where she was in refit, having just taken part in Operation Fork, the British occupation of Iceland. Following the German invasion of Denmark and Norway, Britain occupied Iceland to forestall a German invasion: *Berwick* had landed the marines in Reykjavik and searched the fjords for enemy ships. She sailed again from Birkenhead in August but was damaged in a collision with a merchant ship and returned to harbour for docking and further repairs. She did not rejoin the Home Fleet at Scapa Flow until 22 September.

> "And in about June/July I was appointed to be the sub-lieutenant of a big cruiser HMS *Berwick* and we went out to the Mediterranean. I was in charge of the gunroom of about fifteen midshipmen. We had a terrific range in a ship like that and so we moved about quite a lot, down into the Mediterranean and out into the Atlantic.
>
> "You can imagine that this was about June, I suppose, June 1940 when Italy came into the war, and Italy had a very strong navy, several battleships and cruisers and they were built for Mediterranean warfare, and they could go very fast. We met them once, I think it was in October/November 1940 just to the south of Sardinia. It was one of the very few, big conventional naval actions of the whole war. We had a fleet of about four battleships, six cruisers, two aircraft carriers, and the Italian fleet was equally big but I don't think they had aircraft carriers because they relied upon shore-based aircraft being relatively small distances to fly. This was south of Sardinia and we opened fire at 15 miles range and they opened fire on us and we hit them and they hit us, but no fatal casualties but, of course, the Italians' policy was always to save their fleet and to go full speed back to their Italian base, and this they did and we started to chase them but they were faster, their ships were built for very great speed and they could go 2 or 3 knots faster than British ships and furthermore, the admiral just couldn't let our ships go towards Italy and away from our

> bases at Gibraltar or Malta so we had to be recalled and they went back to Italy, and a bit of stalemate that battle was."

Balme's time in *Berwick* in the Mediterranean, where Italy had joined the war on the Axis side, was rather more exciting than this rather bald account. *Berwick* sailed from the Clyde on 30 October for the Mediterranean where, in the words of the Naval Staff Battle Summary:

> "November was to prove a notable month at sea. In the western part of the Mediterranean, Force H made three important voyages as far as the Narrows, bringing more reinforcements for the Mediterranean Fleet [based at Alexandria], aircraft for Malta and passing military transports through to Malta or Alexandria. On the last cruise some of Vice-Admiral Somerville's force had a running fight with Italian battleships and cruisers".[5]

Berwick sailed from Britain in company with the battleship HMS *Barham*, the cruiser HMS *Glasgow*, and the destroyers *Gallant, Griffin, Greyhound* and *Encounter*, a force designated as Force F, and joined forces based at Gibraltar, which included the fleet aircraft carrier HMS *Ark Royal*. This was part of a series of ten operations between 4 and 14 November, a highly choreographed set of manoeuvres from the western and eastern ends of the Mediterranean that characterised British naval operations at this stage of the war. At Gibraltar Force F joined with Force H and sailed for Malta, where on 10 November they landed stores and troops – *Berwick* alone carried 750 troops. The next day *Berwick* sailed to be part of the close escort of the carrier HMS *Illustrious* for Operation Judgement. *Illustrious* closed on the Italian coast, while the main body of the fleet covered to the south-west, and launched two squadrons of Swordfish torpedo bombing aircraft, which successfully attacked the Italian harbour of Taranto sinking or damaging several ships of the Italian battle fleet. Balme had taken his part in what will ever be evoked as the Battle of Taranto, about which Admiral Cunningham wrote: "Taranto, and the night of November

11–12, 1940, should be remembered for ever as having shown once and for all that in the Fleet Air Arm the Navy has its most devastating weapon." The Fleet Air Arm attack on Taranto was to become the blueprint for the Japanese raid on Pearl Harbour a year later.

Continuing to Alexandria, *Berwick* now joined the cruisers HMS *Glasgow* and HMS *York* and the Australian HMAS *Sydney* of the 3rd Cruiser Squadron and ferried troops to Athens on 15 November. Meanwhile, the Italians still hoped to disrupt the British Mediterranean convoys and on the night of 17 November their battleships *Vittorio Veneto* and *Giulio Cesare* set out to challenge a convoy from Gibraltar that included the aircraft carriers HMS *Ark Royal* and *Argus*, which had aircraft on board to be delivered to Malta. Warned by signal intelligence of the Italian manoeuvre, the British withdrew to prepare, ten days later, a stronger and more elaborate convoy movement, and *Berwick* returned to the Western Mediterranean for Operation Collar. This was a small, fast three-ship convoy bound for Malta and Alexandria, covered by a strong fleet commanded by Admiral James Somerville.

Again the Italians sallied to intercept and the brief Battle of Cape Spartivento ensued. At 09:20 on 27 November *Ark Royal*'s aircraft spotted the enemy some 60 to 75 miles away to the north-east and steering towards the British fleet. Admiral Somerville deployed his forces into several groups, five cruisers in advance of the battleship HMS *Ramillies* and the battlecruiser HMS *Renown*, and the carrier HMS *Ark Royal*, which was operating her aircraft to the south.

At 12:20 the leading cruisers were in range of each other and opened fire at 12½ miles' range. The first Italian salvoes fell accurately and in a few minutes *Berwick* was hit. An 8-inch shell knocked out her Y turret and started a fire that took an hour to subdue. At 12:35 another shell destroyed the aft electrical switchboard in *Berwick* and cut power to that section of the ship, including the X turret, killing seven men and wounding nine others. In the course of the next few minutes fortunes see-sawed. The Italian cruisers started a smokescreen and retired eastwards when the British battlecruiser *Renown* drew into range and threatened to outgun them. They turned again when, at about 13:00, the Italian battleship *Vittorio Veneto* opened fire at 15 miles range. As water spouts erupted around *Berwick* and *Manchester*, it became the turn of the British ships to make smoke and to withdraw to the south-east towards *Ramillies*. Next it was the Italians' turn to flee and in less than an hour the battle was over, with *Berwick* the principal British casualty and a destroyer damaged on the Italian side.

The dead in *Berwick* were Stoker Henry Chissell, Petty Officer Cook Leslie Frost, Leading Sick Berth Attendant Cyril Hulley, Able Seaman John Lightfoot, Able Seaman James MacIlwain, Chief Petty Officer Cook James Styles, and Surgeon Lieutenant William Wildman.[6]

Meanwhile, the convoy had successfully rendezvoused with Admiral Andrew Cunningham's ships from Alexandria and reached its destination safely. While *Berwick* was under repair at Gibraltar she was designated to join a hunting group, Group K, to track down German commerce raiders, and when this order was cancelled she sailed on 21 December to relieve the cruiser HMS *Naiad* as escort for Convoy WS5A.

A page from Balme's scrapbook – bombs dropping near HMS Berwick, 10 November 1940

6

THE FIGHT WITH THE HEAVY CRUISER *HIPPER*

In late December 1940 *Berwick* rendezvoused in mid-Atlantic with Convoy WS5A, a troop convoy from Britain to the Middle East, and on Christmas Day, about 700 nautical miles west of Cape Finisterre, Spain, she briefly fought the German heavy cruiser *Admiral Hipper.* The German had sailed from Germany on 30 November and had broken out into the Atlantic via the Denmark Strait on 6 December. After nearly three weeks' fruitless search *Admiral Hipper* found Convoy WS5A, and thinking that it was a normal trade convoy and not wishing to attack in the dark when torpedo-armed destroyers might be present, *Admiral Hipper* lay off and stalked it through the winter's night. Balme recalled:

> "We met one famous action on Christmas Day. We were off the Bay of Biscay with a convoy of merchant ships and troopships mainly, taking them down to the Cape of Good Hope and then up the other side [of Africa] to Suez and the desert. When suddenly at dawn on Christmas Day, we were all at our action stations and I was in charge of a big gun turret, and suddenly we saw only a few miles away in the dim light a German battlecruiser and we started a real action, both of us firing at each other."

Convoy WS5A – the 'WS' is supposed to stand for 'Winston Special' – was one of a series in 1940–41. Sailing in two sections, it was the only WS convoy to be found and attacked by a German surface raider. Nineteen ships of the slow section sailed from Liverpool and the Clyde on 18 December 1940, including the convoy commodore in the 1926 Belfast-built, Shaw Savill liner SS *Tamaroa*, and the SS *Empire Trooper*, an ex-German liner. Seven ships of the fast section of the convoy followed from Liverpool and the Clyde on 19 December. Five of the merchant ships were carrying supplies for Mediterranean ports and most of the others were troopships carrying reinforcements to the Middle East. The two sections of the convoy rendezvoused on 23 December, by which time the escort consisted of four Flower-class corvettes, the cruisers *Bonaventure*, *Dunedin* and *Berwick*, and the aircraft carriers *Argus* and *Furious*, whose flightdecks were encumbered by cargoes of crated aircraft for Egypt.

The German heavy cruiser Admiral Hipper appeared out of the gloom (Balme)

Balme was in command of B turret of two 8-inch guns when dawn action stations was sounded at 06:15. He recalled that *Berwick*'s commander had given thought, as a Christmas treat, to not ordering dawn action stations and giving the ship's company a lie-in. But, suddenly, the alarm bells rang and the guns went down in elevation, when usually they might have gone up in elevation for range. Balme thought "Crickey a U-boat!" but instead it was *Admiral Hipper* that appeared out of the mist at close range. She had been seen and reported by the corvette *Clematis*, but the first ship seen through the haze from *Admiral Hipper* was *Berwick* on the port bow. *Hipper* – at first thought to be a pocket battleship – opened fire at 06:40 and *Berwick*'s X turret was hit at 07:05. At 07:07 she was hit again below the waterline abreast of B turret, and at 07:10 she was hit for a third time by S1 (starboard, forward, 4-inch gun) mounting, which fired several 8-inch shells that seem to have passed through the hull on the waterline and caused some flooding. However, when *Admiral Hipper* announced her arrival by opening fire, *Berwick* and Balme in his turret was able to reply immediately, and at least one hit was seen to burst on *Hipper*, but by 07:56 when *Hipper* turned and disappeared into the mist, visibility had fallen to half a mile. The flooding in *Berwick* required her to switch from the forward to the after steering position, but at 09:28 the ship's company fell out from actions stations and resumed cursing watches.[7]

Meanwhile, the convoy was ordered to scatter. Now when the elderly cruiser *Dunedin* hove out of the mist, *Admiral Hipper* mistook her for a destroyer and, fearing a torpedo attack, broke off the action and retired into the Atlantic gloom. In the confusion *Admiral Hipper* was unaware that the cruiser *Bonaventure* had also fired off a prodigious amount of 5.25-inch shells at her during the action. The German just had time to score hits on two ships of the convoy, the troopship ship *Empire Trooper* and *Arabistan*. The two carriers also joined the action, though encumbered by many crated aircraft and in atrocious weather, their resources were limited. *Furious* had three Skua dive bombers available and *Argus* had Swordfish torpedo bombers, but *Furious* had no bombs and *Argus* had no torpedoes. The Skuas were flown off as unarmed reconnaissance aircraft, but by the time that the Swordfish had been cross-decked, armed and readied to fly off, there was no sign of *Admiral Hipper* and a thoroughly alarmed Admiralty ordered the carriers to cease their suicidal search. The only beneficiaries of the affair were the Swordfish aircrew, who were provided with an early Christmas lunch in both carriers.

> "At any rate the German battlecruiser withdrew, because I think their instructions were whatever happened they were not to get sunk. They withdrew, we hit them several times and they hit us several times and we had about ten casualties."

Estimates of damage were exaggerated by both sides, but *Berwick* did receive four hits, one of which killed four Royal Marines. However, it was the *Admiral Hipper* that fled from the fray for Brest in German-occupied France.

> "It was, when I got out of my turret and walked down the deck afterwards, it was the first time that I had ever seen dead bodies."

Berwick's dead were Sergeant Charles Painter, Corporal Robert Davison, Marine Denis Broom and Marine Reginald Lyons.

If David Balme's memoir of the Battle of Convoy WS5A is terse, the report rendered by the convoy commodore is laconic in the extreme: his sole comment on an attack by a heavy cruiser and the subsequent action was, "25 Dec, convoy dispersed. 28 Dec, convoy reassembled".

In the aftermath of the battle, *Empire Trooper* was escorted to neutral Ponta Delgada in the Azores by the corvette *Cyclamen*, where she arrived on 28 December. While the rest of the convoy was being reassembled, or made for Gibraltar and Freetown, the cruiser *Bonaventure* found the blockade running 8,200-ton *Baden* – thought to be a supply ship for *Hipper* – who had set herself on fire before she was sunk by the British. *Admiral Hipper*, which was low on fuel, made for Brest in German-occupied France, where she arrived also on 28 December, having found and sunk en route the SS *Jumna*, which had left Convoy OB260 to sail independently.

> "Several shells had hit us, not to damage us very badly but enough to cause casualties, and so we carried on with this convoy but eventually two to three weeks later the Admiralty decided that we must go back to Portsmouth and be repaired from the various damage we had suffered from the German cruiser."

Under these circumstances the safe and timely arrival of the convoy is the aim and, if the fighting around Convoy WS5A was indecisive, the battle was won because all the ships of the convoy reached their destinations. Further, the general failure of the German navy's surface fleet to sink ships increased Hitler's disappointment in the performance of his navy and led to his eventual decision to order its ships to be mothballed or scrapped.

> "And that must have been just about Christmas, no just after Christmas, because the action was on Christmas Day. In the middle of January we turned up at Portsmouth and everybody was paid off because they couldn't afford to have the whole ship's crew doing nothing for several months, and I actually went off to do my sub-lieutenants' courses, which was a marvellous time."

Berwick, after temporary repairs at Gibraltar, returned to Britain in early January 1941 for permanent repairs, which lasted until June 1941. Balme left *Berwick* on arrival in Portsmouth, and was appointed to HMS *Bulldog* on 23 March 1941.

7

HMS *BULLDOG*

Balme's oral memoir continues:

> "At any rate, we [*Berwick*] were damaged and we were sent back home to be repaired, and it was quite a lot of damage and we were always short of officers and men in the Navy and we were sent off to different ships, and it was then that I joined HMS *Bulldog*, which was far the best time that I ever had in the Navy."

HMS *Bulldog* was one of sixteen destroyers, the A- and B-class, ordered in two flotillas for the Royal Navy during the 1930s. Each flotilla consisted of seven ships and one destroyer leader, the latter with slightly enlarged accommodation for the staff of a captain in charge of each flotilla (two additional A-class ships, *Saguenay* and *Skeena*, were built for the Royal Canadian Navy). As ever, the naval staff requirement was overly ambitious and the eventual design was a compromise between cost and capability. Nevertheless, these ships were more heavily armed and had greater range than their prototypes, at the expense of speed. Both classes were armed with four or five 4.7-inch guns in single mountings and with 21-inch torpedoes. At that time, destroyer flotillas alternated between those (the A-class) fitted with ocean minesweeping gear, and the B-class fitted with ASDIC and depth charges. They had very little anti-aircraft capability: the armament was altered during their lives to equip them better for anti-submarine warfare and for anti-aircraft defence. The machinery varied across the classes, but they were capable of a top speed well in excess of 30 knots and a range of 5,000 miles at 15 knots.

A pre-war photograph of HMS Bulldog: she saw service throughout the Second World War (Balme)

Bulldog was ordered on 22 March 1929 from Swan Hunter at Wallsend on the Tyne, under the 1928 Naval Programme. She was laid down on 10 August 1929, launched on 6 December 1930, and completed 8 April 1931 at a cost of £221,408. She displaced 1,360 tons at standard load and 1,790 tons at deep load, was 323 feet in length with a beam of 32 feet 3 inches and a draught of 12 feet 3 inches. She was powered by Parsons geared steam turbines, driving two shafts, which developed a total of 34,000 shaft horsepower and gave a maximum speed of 35 knots. Steam for the turbines came from three Admiralty three-drum boilers. Her peacetime complement was 134 officers and ratings, which increased to 142 in war. *Bulldog* mounted four 4.7-inch guns, whose elevation was only 30 degrees, and two 40-millimetre (2-pounder) anti-aircraft guns. She also carried two quadruple 21-inch torpedo mountings, and a single depth charge rail servicing two throwers. Initially she carried twenty depth charges, but these were increased to thirty-five shortly after the war began, and she was fitted

with Type 119 ASDIC set. By April 1941, when Balme joined her, one torpedo mounting had been replaced by a 3-inch (12-pounder) anti-aircraft gun, but radar had not yet become available.
Also, in an innovation rarely mentioned in histories, *Bulldog* carried radiotelephone equipment and could speak to her consorts by voice, as well as by flag and light.

Bulldog saw service throughout the Second World War on convoy escort duties during the Battle of the Atlantic and in the Arctic. In addition, at 07:15 on 9 May 1945, the German surrender of the Channel Islands was given on the quarterdeck of *Bulldog*, and immediately afterwards all German flags and ensigns were ordered to be lowered. *Bulldog* was also an effective anti-submarine vessel, and her most famous action was the capture of *U-110* in May 1941.

Balme on the bridge of HMS Bulldog in 1941 (Balme)

Destroyers were known as the workhorses of the fleet, and *Bulldog* was no exception. In 1932 she provided disaster relief to the survivors of an earthquake at Lerissos in Greece, and she saw service 1936–38 during the Spanish Civil War enforcing the arms blockade imposed by

Britain and France on both sides in that bloody conflict. She escorted the battleship HMS *Resolution* during the Munich Crisis, was part of the Gibraltar Local Flotilla in the winter of 1938–39, was plane guard for the aircraft carrier HMS *Glorious* in the Mediterranean in March 1939, and in October 1939 was part of a hunting group in the Indian Ocean looking for German surface raiders. In May 1940 *Bulldog* joined the Home Fleet at Scapa Flow and became part of a force hunting for German minelayers in the Skagerrak. There, when the destroyer *Kelly* (Captain Lord Louis Mountbatten) was torpedoed, *Bulldog* towed her to the Tyne for repairs. In June 1940 *Bulldog* took part in Operation Cycle, the evacuation of British troops from Le Havre, and was badly damaged when attacked from the air, but reached Portsmouth under her own steam. Although she was further damaged during an air raid on 24 August, she was at sea again in early September 1940.

Bulldog was refitted at Cammell Laird from 2 January to 18 February 1941, when Commander Joe Baker-Cresswell took command of her and of the 3rd Escort Group.

Bulldog was, Balme recalled:

> "A happy little ship with only about four or five officers and we were leaders of the 3rd Escort Group on North Atlantic convoys. We used to go out from the river Clyde taking the merchant ships up the coast of Scotland then across to Iceland. At Iceland we'd have to go in and refuel, and other destroyers would come and take the convoy on. There'd be about forty or fifty ships in a convoy, a vast mass, you can imagine how it would fill up the entire [Solent], and we would just zigzag along, first to port, then to starboard, trying to confuse any U-boats. There was no radar in those days, but the submarines could be twenty miles out and could follow our masts, the masts of the convoy and could shadow it, whereas we couldn't possibly see the U-boats. We had RAF reconnaissance planes which could patrol around and try and make the U-boats submerge, because once they were submerged they couldn't keep up with the convoy really, but once they were on the

surface, of course, they had great speed. When we got into the difficult zone, south of – between Iceland and Greenland, we'd usually be attacked, once in the early morning and again at midday, say, and then in the evening. Each time the U-boats would probably sink two or three ships and we would hunt for the U-boats, rather unsuccessfully.

"And then early on in the war [in June 1940], we captured Iceland. This was a Danish island, a big island right up north-west of Scotland, near Greenland.

"We captured it and made it a base, so that all our destroyers could refuel there, so ships could be escorted all the way across the Atlantic. The first batch would be taken from Scotland up to Iceland and then the destroyers would go in to refuel, and other destroyers would come out and take the convoy on past Greenland, and then the Canadian navy would come out from Halifax. The merchant ships were in these big convoys or about forty ships, a vast armada of ships, which the U-boats could see from miles away, as you can imagine in clear daylight hours they would see the masts sticking up, they didn't even bother to see hulls, they could see the masts and the direction in which they were going, and they could call other U-boats and they would all concentrate. Remember the convoy was meant to be going at about 8 knots and the U-boats could go 15–20 knots on the surface so they could get to the best possible firing position, then they would submerge and come towards the convoy and just pick off two or three ships at a time. Of course we would counterattack, sometimes with success but usually it was very difficult to pinpoint a U-boat exactly with all those merchant ships around you. You couldn't really leave the convoy for long."

Elsewhere Balme wrote:

"Life in HMS *Bulldog* was the happiest time of the war for me. We had a fine captain, a good crew and just a handful of delightful and efficient officers. In May 1941, not only were we short of ships, but also desperately short of officers and men. In the wardroom we had as watch keepers on this convoy a lieutenant aged 22, myself aged 20, and a RNVR sub-lieutenant. So it was a very tiring life. Four hours on watch, eight hours off, but during those eight hours we had to do our other duties. For instance, in May 1941, I was the navigator, [I was] in charge of the ship's office, and as we were one officer short [the first lieutenant was sick and had been left ashore], I was also doing gunnery control. The most tiring time of all was at night for in the winter months, night was sixteen hours out of twenty-four. We had forty to fifty merchant ships and eight to ten escort vessels and we would all zigzag night and day at a speed of only eight knots. On the bridge was an officer of the watch, a signal man and two lookouts."

However, being navigator was not without its compensations:

"I was navigating officer of the ship at that time so I had a chart room just behind [the bridge] with all the charts and books in and it was a lovely job because you could nip in there and rest and go onto the bridge when you felt like it."

8

THE BATTLE FOR CONVOY OB318

The Battle for Convoy OB318, which reached its climax on 9 May, set Commander Joe Baker-Cresswell and the 3rd Escort Group against Wolfpack West and the notorious Kapitänleutnant Fritz-Julius Lemp and his *U-110*.

Fritz-Julius Lemp was born in Tsingtao, China, which was then a colony of Imperial Germany, on 19 February 1913. His claim to infamy was that on 3 September 1939, on the first evening of the Second World War and while in command of *U-30*, he had sunk the 13,581-ton passenger ship *Athenia*. *Athenia* was outward bound from Glasgow to Montreal carrying more than 1,000 passengers including some 500 Jewish refugees, 469 Canadians, 311 US citizens and 72 British subjects, and 315 crew. She was 60 miles south of Rockall when Lemp sighted her around 16:30 in the afternoon. He claimed that because she was darkened, steering a zigzag course, and well off the normal shipping routes he was justified in thinking that she was an armed merchant cruiser. Lemp tracked *Athenia* for three hours until, at 19:40, he fired two torpedoes, hitting *Athenia*, which began to settle by the stern. Several other ships were in the vicinity and rescued 981 passengers and crew. However, the German liner SS *Bremen*, en route from New York to Murmansk, also received *Athenia*'s distress call but ignored it. News of the sinking made headlines such as 'Empire at War' in outsized red print, and among the dead were twenty-eight US citizens. Fearing that the incident would bring the US into the war, Hitler ordered that *U-30*'s attack should be kept secret.[8] Rather, the Nazi newspaper *Völkischer Beobachter* blamed the loss of the *Athenia* on the British, accusing Winston Churchill, then First Lord of the Admiralty, of sinking the ship in order to turn neutral opinion against Nazi Germany. The full truth did not emerge until the Nuremberg trials in 1946, when Dönitz admitted that *Athenia* had been torpedoed by *U-30* and that the event had been covered up. Lemp was not censured and remained in command of *U-30*, going on to sink, between September 1939 and August 1940, twenty ships of more than 120,000 tons and becoming the seventh U-boat commander to be awarded the Knight's Cross.

In November 1940 Lemp took command of *U-110*, taking with him from *U-30* some of his officers and petty officers. When later, they were interrogated as prisoners of war it was noted that "the petty officers were nearly all men of considerable experience who had served under Lemp on most of the cruises of U-30; he seems to have been unusually successful in retaining his experienced men." He was not so lucky with his more senior officers. The first lieutenant, Oberleutnant zur See Dietrich Loewe, who was also his cousin, was "extremely unpopular with the crew who thought him brainless and inefficient; they looked on him as a Jonah, as the torpedo boat *Lux* in which he was then serving, was lost early in the war, and the destroyer in which Loewe served at Narvik was also sunk ... Loewe was an ardent Nazi and could tolerate no criticism of the Nazi regime. He was also narrow-minded, callous, brutal and a bully. His lack of naval experience was explained by the statement that he had been on sick leave for several months, as he suffered from fainting fits."

The third officer in *U-110* was Leutnant zur See Ulrich Wehrhöfer, who was considered, by the crew, "to be extremely unreliable, and the Chief Petty Officers did not trust him to carry out properly any important observation or calculation ... he gave the impression of possessing moderate intelligence, but of lacking general knowledge." The engineer officer, Oberleutnant Hans Joachim Eichelborn, "was quite a pleasant type and was considered by the crew of 'U 110' to be an excellent engineer ... the son of a country schoolmaster in a small town near Berlin ... he spoke some English and showed no animosity towards Great Britain. [However] he expressed great admiration for Hitler and professed to be convinced of an ultimate German victory, although he was by no means a fanatical Nazi. He was reasonably well educated and a man of some sensibility."

Lemp was delayed by ice in the Baltic and did not sail from Germany on his first operational patrol until 9 March 1941. One of the men who followed Lemp from *U-30* to *U-110* was Georg Högel, a wireless operator and an amateur artist. Despite Dönitz's orders to remove all identification marks from U-boats, Lemp had Högel paint his pet fox terrier, Schnurzl, as a personal emblem on each side of the conning tower. When he saw this, Dönitz liked the idea but still wanted it removed before Lemp went to sea: it was an order that was ignored and a custom that was widely followed throughout the U-boat fleet.

South of Iceland on 15 March, Lemp spotted and started to shadow a convoy of, he estimated, fifteen to twenty steamers with several large tankers and two destroyers. He made the first of several sighting reports to U-boat command and began to broadcast a beacon for other U-boats to home on. The convoy was Convoy HX112, which was carrying war materials and oil from Halifax to Liverpool. On this occasion no wolf pack was formed, but the U-boat attack that developed comprised several experienced U-boat commanders: the convoy escort, the 5th Escort Group, was under the formidable Commander Donald Macintyre in the destroyer HMS *Walker*. Seven ships were torpedoed and five sank, but two U-boats, both commanded by aces, were lost: Joachim Schepke was crushed when the destroyer HMS *Vanoc* rammed his *U-100*, and Otto Kretschmer of *U-99* was fished from the water and taken prisoner by Donald Macintyre's *Walker*.

Lemp also made two attacks on HX112: in the first he set fire to the tanker *Erodona*, but in his second attack he missed with all torpedoes. A few days later Lemp was one of the first U-boats to enter Lorient in German-occupied France, where he learned that besides Kretschmer and Schepke, another U-boat ace, Günther Prien and his *U-47* were missing after attacking another convoy, Convoy OB293, on 7 March 1941.

After three weeks, Lemp left Lorient on 15 April amidst the customary palaver on his second patrol in *U-110.* He had one extra officer: 23-year old Helmut Ecke from Berlin was a war correspondent of the Propaganda Kompanie (PK) whose task was to write stories and record on film the cruise of *U-110.* Although he had been given officer's rank he had never been in a U-boat before, and though he did not want to be regarded as a passenger, all he was trusted with was a turn on watch as conning tower lookout.

Reaching his station west of Ireland in the early hours of 27 April 1941, Lemp found the 2,500-ton cargo ship SS *Henri Mory. Henri Mory,* en route from Bermuda to the UK, was a sitting duck: she was steaming a straight course at 4 knots in fine and clear weather, and she was unescorted because she was deemed too slow to join a convoy. *Henri Mory* was torpedoed and sank in less than four minutes; the master and most of the crew were lost. Lemp found the chief officer and two other survivors in a lifeboat and, after interrogating him, left him with a bottle of cognac and two packets of cigarettes. Lemp had reached a nadir when he wished the chief officer: 'Goodbye, you will be picked up shortly. Tell Winston Churchill there is a war on.'

Hubris followed hard on the heels of this easy success. After several more days of inactivity on 5 May 1941 Lemp heard a broadcast from BdU. A convoy of about fifty ships escorted by fifteen destroyers was forming near the Hebrides. This was Convoy OB318, under its convoy commander, retired Rear-Admiral W. B. Mackenzie. Against it Dönitz could range some nineteen U-boats, designated Wolfpack West – although in the event only a handful of these boats got into position to threaten the convoy. When *U-94* sighted the convoy and made its report, Dönitz ordered *U-110* and the first of five other boats to intercept.

In command of the convoy's escort was Commander Joe Baker-Cresswell. He was born on 2 February 1901 in Mayfair, London, as the younger son of a Guards officer whose family owned land in Northumberland. Joe's first name was Addison, but he never used this. He and his elder brother, John, both joined the Royal Navy, though John was drowned while on picket-boat duty in Portsmouth harbour in 1920. Joe's first ships as a midshipman were the battlecruiser HMS *Tiger*, and then the light cruiser HMS *Castor*, based at Queenstown during the Troubles in Ireland, and the sloop HMS *Veronica*, based in New Zealand in 1924–26 (when he met and married Rona Eileen Vaile). After specialising in navigation Baker-Cresswell was appointed to the minelayer HMS *Adventure* in 1927, to *Veronica* in New Zealand again in 1928–30, and the battleship HMS *Nelson* in 1931–32, followed by three happy years as navigator of the battleship HMS *Rodney*, during which he was twice commended for his skill in piloting that famously unwieldy ship in and out of harbour. Promoted to commander in June 1937, Baker-Cresswell studied on the naval staff course at Greenwich and at the RAF staff college at Andover, before joining General Wavell's staff in Cairo as staff officer joint planning at General Headquarters Middle East. Baker-Cresswell was involved in missions to Turkey and Greece, and for a few months in 1940 he also held the appointment of assistant naval attaché, Ankara. Rear-Admiral Algernon M. Willis reported that Baker-Cresswell had "conducted himself entirely to my satisfaction ... and carried out his duties, which included liaison with the Army and RAF, with considerable ability, much zeal and very tactfully".[9]

Arriving in London a few days before Christmas 1940, Baker-Cresswell went to the Admiralty to seek an appointment at sea:[10]

> "Ten yards short of the door to the office where the person responsible for commanders' appointments resided I met Admiral Sir Percy Noble. That meeting decided the whole course of the rest of the war for me and I often wonder what would have happened if I had entered the Admiralty two minutes later, missed him altogether and entered the door I was making for.
>
> "As it was, I shook him warmly by the hand and congratulated him on his appointment as commander in chief, Western Approaches. We were old friends. Our families knew each other and had friends in common and I had served under him some years before when he commanded the

Second Cruiser Squadron and I was navigating officer of a minelayer in his squadron.

"We discussed families and our respective adventures – I hadn't met him since before the war – and finally I asked him if he could get a command in the Western Approaches. He said: 'Leave it to me, I'll fix it.' And so I didn't go to the appointments office at all.

"A fortnight later, soon after the New Year 1941, I found myself in command of HMS Arrow as Senior Officer of the 3rd Escort Group based at Greenock."

The destroyer *Arrow* was fresh from repairs on the Clyde to her engines, when she rejoined the Home Fleet on 14 January 1941. A month later, when the slightly more modern destroyer *Bulldog* had completed her refit at Cammell Laird in Birkenhead, Baker-Cresswell switched to her. Her camouflage scheme was mauve in the summer (and erroneously known as 'Mountbatten pink') and white in the winter, to which Baker-Cresswell added a jaunty blue and yellow chequered band on the funnel – like the naval numeral flag 'three' – showing that she was part of the 3rd Escort Group (EG3). Unkind remarks were made about Bird's custard tins or Scottish policemen, but EG3 set a fashion for distinguishing marks that others followed. Intended to protect convoys in the North Western Approaches – the North Atlantic between Scotland and Iceland, EG3 in January 1941 consisted of three destroyers, four corvettes, and six trawlers. Baker-Cresswell soon proved himself to be a popular officer and a good leader who moulded EG3 into an efficient and effective force.

In the tide of war that was the Battle of the Atlantic – the longest continuous campaign of the Second World War – more and more U-boats were becoming available to Dönitz. By the spring of 1941 he had moved his headquarters from Germany to Kerneval in France and he was pushing his boats further and further west into the Atlantic, hoping to catch the convoys without their escorts or air cover. The British and Canadians (the USA was not yet in the war) ran convoys with escorts from Canada and Britain, but the escorts' range was limited and there was a gap in the mid-Atlantic. So in April Baker-Cresswell was ordered to base his escort group in Hvalfjord in Iceland in order to extend cover in the ocean south of Greenland and Iceland.

Convoy OB318 was a westbound convoy of thirty-eight ships, either in ballast or carrying trade goods, which had sailed from Liverpool on 2 May 1941 bound for North America and escorted by the 7th Escort Group (EG7), who were to be relieved in mid-ocean by Baker-Cresswell and eight ships of EG3. In Iceland Baker-Cresswell had under his command the destroyers *Bulldog*, *Amazon* and *Broadway*, the Flower-class corvettes *Aubretia*, *Hollyhock* and *Nigella*, and the anti-submarine trawlers *Daneman* and *St Apollo*. *Aubretia*, *Hollyhock* and *Nigella* sailed from Hvalfjord, Iceland, after dark on 6 May and were joined off Reykjavik by *St Apollo*, *Bulldog*, *Amazon* and *Broadway*. Armed merchant cruiser *Ranpura* sailed at 02:00 on 7 May and *Daneman*, which was delayed by a boiler defect, followed. EG3 met Convoy OB318 that evening, and EG7 began to leave to refuel in Iceland.

Though the 3rd Escort Group had only been together a few months, Baker-Cresswell had already welded it into a fighting team. In the next few days, its commanding officers would show that they too had shaped their individual ships into effective warships. One of these was the commander of the new Flower-class corvette *Aubretia* (often misspelled 'Aubrietia' in the records), a Merchant Navy officer, Lieutenant Commander Vivian Funge Smith RNR. Smith had previously commanded another ship of EG3, the anti-submarine trawler *St Apollo*, and could always be relied upon to 'do the right thing.'[11] Another of these was the four-funnelled, former-USN, lend-lease destroyer, *Broadway* commanded by Lieutenant Commander Thomas Taylor RN, who had been passed over for promotion in the interwar years.

After *U-94*, commanded by Herbert Kuppisch, had reported Convoy OB318 to BdU on 7 May 1941, Dönitz called up reinforcements while Kuppisch submerged ahead of the ships. He had been in command of *U-94* for a year, with an experienced crew who were on their fifth patrol together, and though hunted intermittently by EG7 for several hours and, having let the leading escorts pass overhead, shortly after 23:00 Kuppisch fired at close range on the ships in the centre of the convoy, hitting the 10,000-ton Holt steamship *Ixion* and the 5,600-ton Norwegian *Eastern Star*.[12] By the glare of burning ships the sloop *Rochester*, commanded by Lieutenant Commander Conway Benning Allen, saw Kuppisch's periscope and attacked at once. Over the next few hours *Rochester*, joined by *Bulldog* and *Amazon* of EG3, dropped ninety-eight depth charges, which damaged *U-98* and forced Kuppisch to drop astern of the convoy and call off his attack.[13]

However, it was 16:00 on 8 May before Baker-Cresswell caught up with his convoy, and he was able to set a screen for the night. He adopted his favourite disposition, with an ASDIC line of three destroyers and two corvettes zigzagging together ahead of the convoy: in the order (port to starboard) *Amazon*, *Hollyhock*, *Bulldog*, *Nigella*, and *Broadway*. He ordered the trawler *Angle* (EG7) on the portside of the convoy and the corvette *Aubretia* to starboard, to tuck them into the wing column so that should a U-boat penetrate the screen, they would be ready to pounce. The trawlers *Daneman* and *St Apollo* were to be what he called the fullbacks, to round up any stragglers from the convoy and to escort any ship that dropped back.

Dusk fell about 22:30 when Baker-Cresswell sent off *Amazon* and *Bulldog* to make a search out to 10 miles on either side of the convoy. He wrote:

> "With their protective covering [camouflage] in that half-light they would have a good chance of sighting a U-boat ... but they sighted nothing and returned to their night screening positions ... So we settled down for the night as we had so often done before, feeling that the situation was in hand, that everyone knew what to do, that all ships were correctly stationed and lookouts were alert."

Baker-Cresswell turned in about 23:30 with an easy mind. What he did not know was that earlier that day, Lemp, on the surface, had sighted the smoke of Convoy OB318 on his port bow, and commenced to shadow from a position about 15 miles ahead. *Broadway* must have only just missed seeing *U-110* in her search.

Now *U-201*, commanded by Adalbert Schnee, joined the fray and next morning, 9 May, Lemp and Schnee rendezvoused and conferred by loudhailer. They agreed that Lemp as senior officer would attack first, submerged and by daylight, and that Schnee would attack half an hour later when the convoy had been thrown into confusion by Lemp's attack. Lemp disregarded his officers, who would have preferred him to wait until nightfall, when the escort might be expected to have left to refuel and the convoy would have become easier prey. Lemp submerged and let the convoy come on. His position was further west than any U-boat attack had previously been made from, and it is likely he was anxious for action. He was tired after three weeks at sea, disturbed by the loss of so many of his fellow aces, frustrated his own lack of success in his previous patrol, and exasperated by his meagre achievements in this patrol.

EG3 should indeed have left the convoy, but Baker-Cresswell had an intuition that there were U-boats still about, and, after asking the ships of his escort group what their fuel endurance was, he had decided to stay another few hours. About the time that Lemp and Schnee were conferring, Baker-Cresswell ordered EG3 to take up its day formation, and at 08:00 he received the fuel reports. Balme, as his navigator, worked out they could stay with the convoy until 16:00 and would then have to leave in order to reach Iceland with no more than a minimum of oil and coal left. No U-boat had ever made an attack as far west as OB318's present position. As Balme recalled:

> "So now we come to the great day of the 9th May 1941. We were attacked by U-boats at about midday, it was a beautiful sunny day, I remember that, calm, just great big Atlantic rollers, blue sky, the sun and I was on the bridge."

Balme had kept the morning watch (from 4 am to 8 am) and was feeling good. He had had a shower and breakfast and spent a couple hours resting in his charthouse, when about midday he had gathered with other officers, as was their custom, on the bridge of *Bulldog*. She was leading the convoy on a south-westerly heading. Many accounts of the day say that Baker-Cresswell was about to calculate his noon position, taking the altitude of the sun using his sextant.[14]

Three miles away on the starboard side of the convoy, Lemp, now submerged, was surprised to see though his periscope quite so many escorts still about the convoy, but he decided to continue his attack and ordered four torpedoes to be readied. When he had closed to within a few hundred yards of the convoy's starboard side he fired his first torpedo at 11:58, which hit the 5,000-ton British *Esmond*. A few seconds afterwards, his second torpedo hit the 2,600-ton *Bengore Head*, but Lemp missed his third target and was looking for a fourth target as he swung the small attack periscope around. He was shocked to see the bow wave of a corvette headed straight at him and fewer than 800 yards away.

In *Bulldog* Baker-Cresswell was looking back at the convoy when he saw the columns of water shoot up into the air and for a second he could not believe his eyes. A torpedo attack almost within sight of Greenland! It was obvious that a U-boat had penetrated the screen from a position between *Broadway* and *Aubretia*. How had *Broadway* failed to detect it? A moment afterwards *Aubretia* hoisted a flag indicating that she had an ASDIC contact. It was the situation that Baker-Cresswell had foreseen when designing the screening disposition: tucked in close to the starboard wing column of the convoy, an attacking U-boat had not noticed *Aubretia*.

At 12:01, Able Seaman William Rutledge, the ASDIC operator in *Aubretia*, reported to his captain, Vivian Funge Smith, that he could hear torpedoes running, and he quickly picked up a contact bearing 350 degrees at 1,000 yards. He almost immediately lost contact again as *Aubretia*'s helm was put hard over and she increased speed to run down at full speed on the bearing of the contact. Next, HMS *Broadway* obtained a contact at 12:03 at close range and dropped one depth charge set to 150 feet and then hauled off while *Aubretia* charged in. As Lemp ordered *U-110* to dive deeper, *Aubretia* passed over him and dropped a salvo of ten depth charges at 12:06 set for 100 feet and 225 feet, and these caused great damage to *U-110*. At 12:10 *Aubretia* stopped engines so she could listen on her ASDIC, and crept forward slowly. At 12:15 *Broadway* saw a swirl of broken water, turned towards, and increased sped to 18 knots. Next, at 12:23½, *Aubretia* dropped a well-placed second salvo of depth charges, set for 150 feet and 385 feet. Lemp's *U-110* was bracketed by the blast and her crew were flung off their feet, the main lights went out, dials and gauges were shattered, and Lemp smashed his head on the deck.[15]

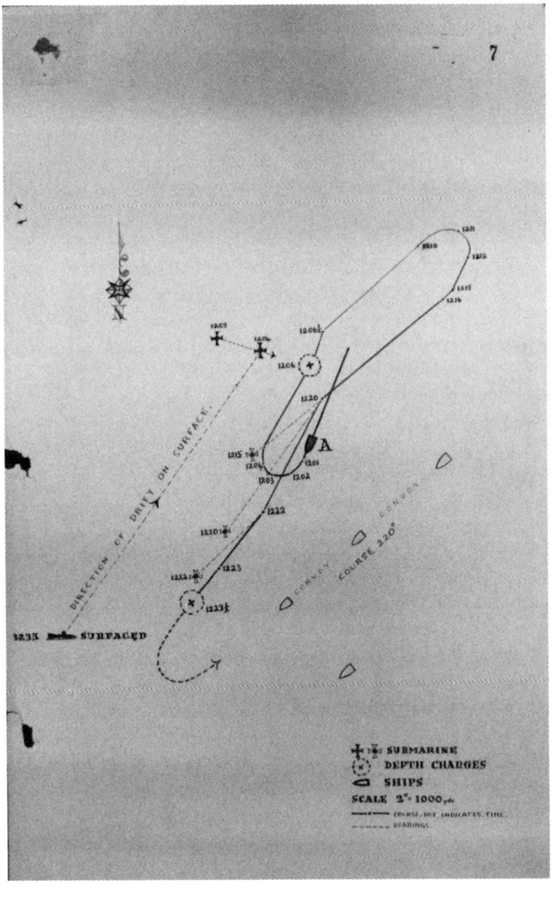

Aubretia's plot of the hunt for U-110

As a thin trickle of blood ran down Lemp's face, his crew reported that the hydroplanes and rudder were not responding, the electric motors had seized, that chlorine gas was seeping from cracked battery cells, and that the handles controlling the high-pressure air for blowing tanks had sheared off. There was no way of telling what depth the boat had reached, but the single remaining – and unreliable – gauge showed that the boat was at 300 metres depth and sinking. Lemp ordered all emergency air to be blown when a sudden and distinctive rocking motion told him that *U-110* had already broken surface. Lemp ordered, "All hands to abandon ship as fast as possible!"

Broadway seems to have been first to see the conning tower break the surface of the sea, in the middle of the flurry of white water stirred up by *Aubretia*'s depth charges, and her captain, Thomas Taylor, decided to ram. In *Bulldog*, Baker-Cresswell was angry that he had lost two ships from the convoy and the sight of a U-boat on the surface filled him with blind rage that made him also determined to ram and sink the German. He was just about to give the order "Prepare to ram!" when the red mist of his anger cleared.

Lemp rushed to the bridge of *U-110*, where he was shocked to see not one but two destroyers, *Bulldog* and *Broadway*, bows-on and charging towards him. Further off he could see a third warship, *Aubretia*. In *Bulldog*, Baker-Cresswell saw men streaming out of the conning tower and supposed that they were abandoning ship, but as the U-boat's hull lifted out of the water, men began to cluster around the gun. "Good God!" thought Baker-Cresswell, "They are going to fight it out on the surface," and he turned *Bulldog* to bring her all guns to bear and ordered, "Open fire!"

Balme was *Bulldog*'s gunnery control officer and he recalled that at 400 yards:

> "In those days we did not have sophisticated control systems and my job, as gunnery control officer, was to call up the three 4.7-inch guns on my telephone headset, give them a bearing and range and tell them to open fire independently."

In fact, the first gun to fire was the 3-inch fitted amidships, which hit the U-boat's conning tower. Seeing men now jumping into the sea, Baker-Cresswell suddenly had another thought and exclaimed, "By God! We'll do a *Magdeburg*!"[16] "In a flash of memory," he remembered what he had learned at Greenwich a few years before, that the Russians had driven a German cruiser, *Magdeburg*, aground in the Baltic in 1914 and captured codebooks that were afterwards given to the British.[17] Later he jested that his words on the bridge of *Bulldog* were "as epoch-making as some of Churchill's sayings".

Baker-Cresswell ordered, "Cease fire!" and then, "Full speed astern!" and stopped 100 yards off *U-110*. He then flashed by light to *Broadway* "Keep clear!" When this had no effect he seized the microphone of the loudhailer, which on a calm day could carry sound for a mile, and yelled, "Do not ram! I intend to board." To Lieutenant Walter Higgs, RNVR, who was still firing a Lewis gun over Baker-Cresswell's head "with such an appalling noise" he snarled, "Put that bloody thing down!"[18]

In *Broadway* Taylor saw men pour out of the conning tower, and to him some appeared go for the gun while others held their arms up in surrender. However, later Baker-Cresswell mused, "Taylor very nearly ruined the whole thing ... he ignored all my signals ... and quite likely ignored my signal to cease fire."[19] A German was hit by a burst from a Hotchkiss gun from *Broadway* and knocked overboard, about the same time that the shock from *Broadway*'s 4-inch gun shattered the glass windows of her bridge and made Taylor's ramming attempt 'slightly in error': the U-boat was slowly turning her stern towards *Broadway* and Baker-Cresswell reckoned that she would be badly placed and the two ships would be end-on at the moment of impact. *Broadway* was sluggish in answering her helm (or Taylor late in giving the order) and she hit the German's hydroplane (a horizontal fin), which sliced open her port forward fuel tank. Fuel oil poured into the sea, and *Broadway*'s port propeller was badly bent as the two ship disengaged. As *Broadway* slid past within a few feet of the U-boat, Taylor, let go two depth charges set to 100 feet. This, he claimed later, was done in order to hasten the Germans' departure.

Balme recalled events slightly differently:

> "And then suddenly at 12:30 precisely [12:01 according to Baker-Cresswell's report of proceedings] there were two big explosions and two ships were hit and when once the ships were hit, a merchant ship, they sink very quickly, in a matter of five or ten minutes, and they heeled over and the crew get into the boats as best they can or jump into the water. We immediately turned the convoy away from the attack and headed the escorts toward the attack, and started looking for the submarine with our ASDIC machine, which would pick them up at about one mile range underwater.
>
> "Well, we got the contact alright and started dropping depth charges, and it was all very successful, one of those days when everything worked right, the right depth set on the depth charges and so, as we were looking out astern, suddenly we saw the U-boat breaking surface, and the conning tower came up and then the whole hull was on the water. We opened fire with all our guns, machine guns and pom-poms, small 3-inch shells, must have made a devastating noise on the hull and cause great panic amongst the German crew. They all jumped overboard."

Baker-Cresswell, remembering his game-shooting etiquette, signalled to *Aubretia*, "This is your bird."

U-110 lies under the guns of HMS Bulldog as she lowers a boat (Balme)

9

THE DEATH OF FRITZ-JULIUS LEMP

U-110 had broken surface at 12:35 about 800 yards off *Bulldog*'s port beam, when *Bulldog* opened fire with all her medium and small calibre guns, and one 3-inch shell was seen to strike the conning tower. Men were indeed seen to be abandoning the submarine.

Later, as a prisoner of war, Helmut Ecke told his interrogators that during the attack he had been ordered out of *U-110*'s control room. The next thing he heard was the tremendous explosion of a depth charge, which he described as far louder and more terrifying than anything he had ever heard. He staggered to the control room, where Lemp immediately ordered him over the side. The next thing he remembered was swimming in the sea. He had on leather breeches and boots and he was not able to inflate his rubber lifebelt, but he was a good swimmer and managed to keep afloat, although he swallowed a great quantity of water and oil.

Lemp, now in the conning tower of the U-boat, passed the order from his place on the bridge to his first lieutenant, Dietrich Loewe, and his engineer, Hans-Joachim Eichelborn, who were in the control room, "Open the vents!" in order to scuttle *U-110*. Lemp remained on the bridge until everyone was out of the boat and, Loewe recalled, when the water was "one meter above the base of the conning tower" and he was certain that *U-110* was sinking, he and then Lemp jumped into the water.

Bulldog stopped within 100 yards of the U-boat, and to Baker-Cresswell, who noted that the U-boat was down by the stern and had a slight list to port, she did not appear to be sinking. There was no sign of a white flag and when two men seemed to be about to man the submarine's forward gun, fire was again opened from a Lewis gun. Two or three men were hit. "My object," wrote Baker-Cresswell, "was to keep the crew rattled. They already appeared dazed and uncertain what to do." However, Baker-Cresswell was clear that: "Everyone was firing at the conning tower and not at the men in the water."[20]

His next orders were, "Away armed boarding party!" and, turning to Balme, "Right, sub, you take the seaboat!"

He added, "Get on board as quickly as you can. I think she is completely abandoned but there may be one or two left on board. Get hold of the signal books first and then anything else useful you can take away."

Balme recalled the moment:

> "One of the corvettes, HMS *Aubretia*, which actually made a very accurate attack, picked up the survivors, bundled them down below quickly so that they couldn't see what was going on, and *Bulldog* ordered her ship's boat away, and I was in charge, and the captain said to me, 'Get whatever you can out of her, documents, books, charts, and get the wireless settings, anything like that'."

He wrote to Roskill:[21]

> "I do not think that I had ever before seen a boat lowered in *Bulldog* at sea and certainly not when we got into harbour [as] we were all too tired ever to practise things like that. However the boat was lowered all right and both ends dropped when we slipped, which was a relief. The weather was calm, but with the usual big Atlantic rollers."

Most references say that there were nine men in the whaler, but Baker-Cresswell makes clear in his post-war account that he sent across "a signalman *and* a wireless telegraphist."[22] The tenth man was William Pollock, who belonged to a Special Signals Unit based at Liverpool that had been established to develop the use of direction finding equipment and he was in *Bulldog* to teach its use. He was on the bridge of *Bulldog* when Baker-Cresswell gave the order to send a boarding party to *U-110* and the acting first lieutenant, John Aitken, said to him, "Pollock, I'd like you to volunteer." The idea was that he should see if the U-boat carried similar equipment to that which he was using.[23]

Meanwhile, oil from *Broadway* was spreading over the surface of the water. In the water and covered by oil, Loewe and Lemp realised that their boat was not going under, and as they saw the conning tower of the boat lift high out of water, Lemp shouted to Loewe, "Let's swim back on board!" However, the men in the water and the U-boat were affected differently by the wind: the men were relatively stationary in the oily water, and while the U-boat's high conning acted like a sail and drove her downwind, one engine (it was discovered later) was running slow ahead, and the wheel was jammed to starboard. She had already moved too far off for anyone to swim back. Loewe turned and swam towards one of the British ships, *Aubretia*, and he lost contact with Lemp.

In *Bulldog*, Baker-Cresswell watched as the whaler was rowed across the 100 yards of heaving water, and he did not recall any shots being fired from it. The Atlantic swell was breaking over the U-boat's slender hull, and it seemed to him that Balme waited his opportunity to row straight for the broadest part of the hull, immediately before the conning tower, when the whaler was lifted by a wave and smashed down on the U-boat's casing, where it was broken in pieces. Seeing this, Baker-Cresswell ordered *Broadway*, which as a US-built ship had a motor boat rather than a rowing boat, "Send boat to stand by my boarding party."

Balme's account is slightly different. Looking across the gap between *Bulldog* and the U-boat, Balme too could see how the German submarine was lying, trimmed down slightly by the stern and with a slight list to port, and he realised that it was being blown downwind.

Appreciating the need for haste, Balme steered the whaler for the nearer, weatherside of the U-boat, rather than the leeside where there would be more shelter. Though he could not be sure, by the time he reached the U-boat, the crew had now all abandoned ship, and were in the water.

Later Balme told Roskill:

> "We only had about two hundred yards to pull and I brought the whaler alongside the bows of the U-boat. The bowman jumped on board and held the whaler while I stumbled for'ard over oars, etc. and got out. While boarding parties are dressed up with revolvers, etc. one had seldom practised with or used one. I suppose I may have fired a few shots with one from the quarterdecks of various ships, but I doubt if the sailors of the boarding party had ever used one at all. However, with revolver in hand I walked along the slippery deck aft to the conning tower."

Aubretia's second, successful attack on *U-110* had put her ASDIC out of action, and she drew off to make repairs. As she did so she began to rescue men from the water. The first survivors she picked up were from SS *Esmond*'s boats. "As they came up the scrambling nets on the port side of *Aubretia*," Funge Smith wrote, "*U-110* bobbed to the surface on the port quarter with *Bulldog* and *Broadway* in close attendance. A spontaneous cheer swept over the ship in which men from the *Esmond* were probably the most vociferous. Our gun's crew were, to their disgust, deprived of chucking a few bricks by the range being foul."[24]

Aubretia, "who could always be relied upon to do the right thing without orders",[25] now began picking up the German survivors, who were all hustled below decks even before Balme set out from *Bulldog* in her whaler.[26] Funge Smith wrote, 'Few had much kick left in them. They were promptly stripped and given a blanket. One who either by design or accident spat in the face of a petty officer was promptly pushed back overboard till he should board in a more proper manner.'[27] *Aubretia*'s first lieutenant, Barry Sheen, reported:[28]

> "After the second attack had forced the submarine to the surface, we stood by to pick up enemy survivors. Some fifteen to twenty were picked up on the starboard side and the remainder in ones and twos on the port side.
>
> "There were one or two lifesaving apparatus floating by, about ½ cable on either beam. During the rescue work it was noticed that few were wearing the special apparatus (sic) the majority wore inflated life jackets. Of those which came sufficiently near the ships side for heaving lines to be thrown, about two were obviously dead, and made no motion even when lines were dropped on their heads or hands.
>
> "When the last of those near the ship had been taken inboard, I went up on to the bridge and reported to the Captain that all those displaying any signs of life had been got in board; and that two visible on the starboard quarter we had judged as dead, they having made no movement at all. The captain said he would turn to starboard so as to pass close to these men, and to make certain that they were lifeless.
>
> "On the ship being brought about, and manoeuvred close to the floating men it was obvious that they were lifeless. At the same time I sighted four or five other men astern to starboard; as these were approached I could see that they were all wearing their life saving apparatus; they were floating in an upright position their heads sunk forward between their arms, which were raised chest high and bent at the elbows. One man passed under our stern as the ship hove to, and somehow managed to catch a rope around him so that we could have him on board. He was wearing the apparatus but the face piece was not adjusted so that he must have swallowed a good deal of water. He was obviously suffering from severe shock and died a short while later."

Besides the survivors from *Esmond*, *Aubretia* had taken on board thirty-four oil-soaked survivors of *U-110*, two of whom died later. Lemp was not among them.

(Much later it was realised in *Aubretia* that, by curious coincidence, Barry Copeland, the chief officer of *Esmond*, had been third mate of *Athenia*, sunk by Lemp on the first day of the war, and that Copeland had the distinction of having served in and survived the sinking of two ships by the same U-boat commander.[29])

The oil-soaked Germans about to be rescued from the water by HMS Aubretia (Balme)

Funkgefreiter or Telegraphist Heinz Wilde, one of *U-110's* four wireless operators, remembered floating so long in the water that he thought he was going to freeze to death, but being helped up a scrambling net in his rapidly weakening state to board *Aubretia*, where the British seamen tried to help him stand up before stripping him naked, wrapping him in a blanket, and massaging him warm. Helmut Ecke of the PK, who had swallowed mouthfuls of oily seawater, vomited on deck, which an officer found 'very, very funny' and started to whistle an ironic *Deutschland Über Alles*.[30]

According to *Aubretia*'s report of proceedings, the last German was plucked from the water at 14:30 – so that the last to be picked up had been in the water some two hours. At 14:32 *Broadway* reported an underwater contact. *Aubretia* joined the hunt and at 14:37 she also picked up a contact. This was possibly Schnee in *U-201* making his escape after attacking the convoy. This new hunt lasted for more than an hour until the contact faded at 15:50. *Broadway* and *Aubretia* then formed a screen around *Bulldog* and later that evening *Aubretia* transferred her prisoners to *Amazon* and took the Germans to Hvalfjord.

Baker-Cresswell was the first to ask what happened to Lemp. The German prisoners were transferred again, this time to *Bulldog*, and two days later she was on passage from Iceland to Scapa Flow, when Baker-Cresswell had Eichelborn, the U-boat's engineer, who he mistook for the second-in-command, brought to the bridge. They spoke in Baker-Cresswell's halting German and Eichelborn's 'much better English,' and when asked about his captain, Eichelborn said 'that they were swimming about together but that when he looked around later there was no sign of Lemp. He thought he had been drowned but did not know if he had been hit.'

In the 1950s Baker-Cresswell and Stephen Roskill corresponded with members of Lemp's family about the return of Lemp's Iron Cross, when there were no recriminations about the manner of his death.[31] It was presumed that Lemp had drowned. Even the propaganda officer Ecke, who believed his own propaganda and claimed that he had been shot at in the water and did not expect to be rescued by the British, supposed that Lemp intended to commit suicide by going down with the U-boat and that he had thrown himself over the side and deliberately allowed himself to be carried away.[32]

Forty years later the British were accused of shooting Lemp in the water but there is no evidence for this. The accusation was first made in 1977 in a book by a two British journalists, Costello and Hughes,[33] but theirs is a popular history with sources listed and a bibliography but no footnotes or endnotes so it is not clear on what evidence they based their charge. Nevertheless, it has been repeated down the years, sometimes with added, graphic verisimilitude in an otherwise generally reliable work of reference but that does not make it any less untruthful.[34] Significantly, when the BBC interviewed the German survivors of *U-110* for a television programme in 2002, no one made any allegation that Lemp had been murdered,[35] and when Jonathan Dimbleby wrote his account of the Battle of OB318, he concluded that Lemp 'like 14 of his crew was presumed to have drowned.'[36] Nor have other respected writers who have written about the capture of *U-110* repeated any such unsubstantiated claim: e.g. Patrick Beesly (1977),[37] Winton (1988),[38] Kahn (1991),[39] and Hugh Sebag-Montefiore (2000).[40]

However, in 1981 Balme heard that the German weekly *Bild am Sonntag* had published a story on 5 April 1981 that one of the sailors in the whaler 'had seized a machine pistol which hung round his neck' and shot Lemp. Balme's friend and neighbour in Lymington, Patrick Beesly, contacted the newspaper's editor, who investigated the weekly's own story. The editor interviewed Balme and some of the German survivors of *U-110* and on 30 August 1981 a retraction was printed. The editor accepted that the British boarding party was armed with First World War vintage Webley .45 revolvers and not rifles or sub-machine guns, and therefore could not have shot anyone with a 'machine pistol' (a German weapon). He also accepted that light firing was still taking place when Balme's whaler was approaching the U-boat, but that Balme never saw Lemp, still less identified who he was among the oil-soaked survivors in the sea, and *Bild am Sonntag* accepted that Lemp had suffered a heart attack or drowned.

When the story about Lemp having been shot in the water reappeared on the letters page of the *Daily Telegraph* in 1988, Balme wrote:[41]

> "I was the officer in charge of *Bulldog's* boarding party when we captured the Enigma cipher machine from *U-110* on May 9, 1941. Neither I nor any member of my party saw or shot Kapitän Lemp. No shots were fired by the boarding party. During 1981 the German Sunday newspaper *Bild am Sonntag*

> ran a weekly series on the Battle of the Atlantic, also saying that I had shot Lemp. The late Patrick Beesly (the expert on Naval Intelligence) immediately took the matter up with the editor and the newspaper corrected the matter."

The German newspaper had accepted that the accusation was false, and the last word must be left with Balme, who told the newspaper's readers that the feeling of the prisoners from *U-110* when they were interrogated in *Bulldog* and in London was that Lemp committed suicide in the water.

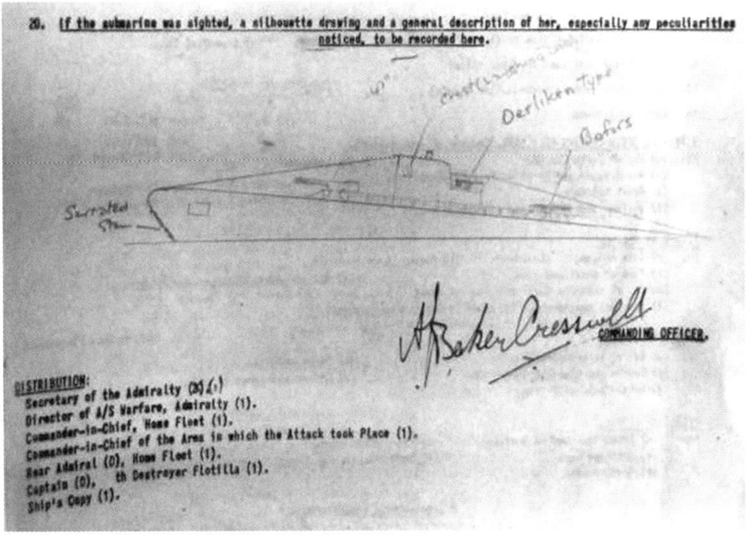

20. If the submarine was sighted, a silhouette drawing and a general description of her, especially any peculiarities noticed, to be recorded here.

A. Baker Cresswell
COMMANDING OFFICER.

DISTRIBUTION:
Secretary of the Admiralty (1).
Director of A/S Warfare, Admiralty (1).
Commander-in-Chief, Home Fleet (1).
Commander-in-Chief of the Area in which the Attack took Place (1).
Commander-in-Chief (D), Home Fleet (1).
Rear Admiral (D), Home Fleet (1).
Captain (D), th Destroyer Flotilla (1).
Ship's Copy (1).

Baker-Cresswell's first sight of his enemy: U-110 carries Lemp's personal crest showing the laughing dog (a caricature of his own pet)

10

THE RANSACK OF *U-110*

Balme's official report reads:

> "At 12:45 9th May, I left *Bulldog* in charge of a boarding party to board an enemy submarine which had surfaced. The crew consisted of 6 seamen, 1 telegraphist and 1 stoker. [He omitted to mention Pollock.] *Bulldog* was lying to windward of U-boat and there was a heavy swell running so to save valuable time I made for the weather side (Port). There were numerous holes in the conning tower casing caused by *Bulldog*'s 3" and Pom-pom. As no small arm fire was opened up at the whaler from the U-boat, I was fairly confident that there was no one in the conning tower.
>
> "We rowed over, only about half a mile to row and I waited in the stern to go alongside, the bowman got out onto the U-boat and held the bow onto the hull of the U-boat."

Balme clambered over the oarsmen to reach the bow of the whaler, and climbed with some difficulty on to the curved sides of the U-boat: it was like walking on a large, slippery rugby ball while being sluiced with water.

> "I jumped out and was on the deck, and with my revolver in my hand I walked down the deck to the conning tower, and then I had to holster my revolver for I had to climb up three ladders to get from the hull to the top of the conning tower, outside in

the open, and of course there was nobody there in the conning tower when I arrived, they'd all jumped overboard.

Mindful perhaps of what had happened to Robert Carr when *Ivanhoe* had boarded the refugee ship *Las Perlas* off Palestine, Balme put away his revolver. At the top of the conning tower Balme was very surprised to find that the hatch leading downwards was closed tight but, on turning a wheel, the hatch sprung open as soon as a clip was released:

> "The hatch down was closed tight. (This hatch was 18" to 24" in diameter, spherical surface with wheel for screwing down; on unscrewing this the hatch sprung open as soon as a clip was released). I didn't think there was anybody down below, but I holstered my revolver and started climbing down [inside] the three ladders. This was a very nasty moment 'cos both my hands were occupied with the rungs of the ladder going down ... and I was a sitting target to anyone down below."

Climbing down the ladder to the lower conning tower, Balme found a similar hatch, also closed: then and later it seemed very strange to Balme that the hatches were not left open if it was intended that the U-boat was to be scuttled:

> "This was the nasty moment, one looked down below and wonder how many Germans there were there. I went down the ladder to the lower conning tower where there was a similar closed hatch. On opening this hatch I found the control room deserted! Hatches leading forward and aft were open and all lighting on. On the deck there was a large splinter from the conning tower. There was a slight escape of air in the control room but no sign of chlorine so gas-masks which had been taken were now discarded.
>
> "I just couldn't see exactly [but] the U-boat seemed to be in reasonable good order. Anyway I got down, right down to the control room, down to the bottom of the last ladder and there

> was nobody there, so I immediately went right for'd and right aft with my revolver in my hand to see if there was anybody about. There was nobody there at all. So I called down my boarding party, and we started ransacking all the treasures of the U-boat."

Balme had felt very vulnerable entering the U-boat feet-first: Now, standing in the control room, the most eerie feeling was the almost complete silence, a silence only broken by an ominous hissing sound that was either the sound of compressed air escaping from a tank or of water leaking into the hull and the occasional of distant depth charges. The secondary lighting gave a rather dim, ghostly effect. The U-boat had a 15-degree list to port and there was a plopping noise as she rolled in the Atlantic swell. Inside the U-boat hatches leading forward and aft were open and swinging to and fro as the U-boat rolled. Lying on the deck was a large metal splinter, presumably from damage caused by the British gunfire. The U-boat had obviously been abandoned in great haste as books and gear were strewn about:[42]

> "The lights were still on and everything was lying around just as if one had arrived at someone's house after breakfast, before they had had time to make beds, etc., coats were thrown around, bunks half made, etc. There was complete silence in the U-boat except for the continual thud of our own depth charges. This was a most unpleasant sound, especially when it got closer, as one expected the U-boat to be blown up at any moment. One was accustomed to dropping depth charges but not hearing them and this caused a most unpleasant sensation. A most unpleasant and frightening noise."

Speed in searching the U-boat was now essential, as Balme felt sure that the scuttling charges would go off sooner or later. It was, he remembered:

> "The first quick look around below took about 5 minutes after which I shouted up the conning tower to Pollock to signal *Bulldog* [using hand-held semaphore flags] 'Nobody on board. All clear'."[43]

However:

> "Our whaler was carried on to the U-boat by the swell and was now firmly lodged between the conning tower and the steel guard rails; it was eventually a total loss."

Broadway was ordered to lower a motor boat to stand by *Bulldog*'s boarding party:

> "A chain of men was formed to pass up all books charts etc. As speed was essential owing to the possibility of the U-boat sinking (although dry throughout) I gave orders to send up ALL books, except obviously reading books, so consequently a number of comparatively useless navigational books etc. were recovered. All charts were in drawers under the chart table in the control room; there were also some signal books, log books etc. here."

Balme sent another message via Pollock to *Bulldog* that the U-boat seemed seaworthy and towable, and requested that an ERA (engine room artificer) be sent over to see if any machinery would work. Using *Broadway*'s boat, *Bulldog* sent across her engineer officer, Lieutenant Commander (E) George Dodds, and two ERAs:

> "Another boat load had arrived by this time, with the Engineer Officer, Gunner (T) and party. [The Gunner (T) probably came later in the day.] They were sent to see if they could stop the port motor, but having turned all the switches they found they could neither do that nor start the starboard motor. They did however collect some further important documents."

On board the submarine, while Balme and his team continued their search, Dodds and his party carried out an inspection. They evaluated the damage in the machinery spaces aft in the boat, trying from first principles to see if they could find out how things worked and perhaps increase the boat's buoyancy. Dodds' son wrote about this:[44]

> "No one had submarine experience and they could not read the German tallies and instructions, and they were fearful of opening cocks or altering settings that might make things worse. All aboard were convinced that scuttling charges had been set that might go off at any time. The pressure waves from depth charge explosions hit the hull with the noise of great hammers. At one point in his search, Dodds went aft and got stuck in a watertight door which swung to and trapped him. Balme saw the Chief Engineer's plight and wrote much later that he would 'never forget the sight of the Chief stuck in the watertight door. It must have been very painful to him but it was extremely funny to see the look on his face, with the depth charges exploding all around and he firmly stuck in the doorway.' The humour of the situation was only apparent to the 20 year-old; Dodds' own recollection was only of great fear, until he was able to open the door again and free himself.
>
> "The Chief Engineer found the pressure hull of the submarine dry, although buckled in the aft compartments; some water was leaking in and air was escaping from the buoyancy tanks, bubbling eerily from inside the boat into the sea. The hydroplanes, electric motors and rudder were out of action, oil was leaking from a damaged fuel tank and gas from a damaged battery."

However, the extent of the damage to the boat seemed to be rather less than reported by prisoners who, later under interrogation, believed and reported that the boat had been wrecked internally. Even with all the switches put to the same position on the port side as on the starboard side, the motor would still not stop. The bilges were dry, and the pressure hull watertight, but there was the bubbling noise of an air leak or an open vent somewhere aft. No one had sufficient submarine experience to attempt to blow the after tanks and no one could read

German or understood the technical German, and no one had any experience of operating a submarine. Convinced he was unable to improve the U-boat's buoyancy or seaworthiness, Dodds and his men joined Balme and the others in rummaging the U-boat.

However, Balme's fear did not stop his search:

> "Meanwhile the telegraphist went to the W/T [wireless-telegraphy] office, just forward of the control room on starboard side. This was in perfect condition, apparently no attempt having been made to destroy any books or apparatus. Here were found C.B's. [confidential books], signal logs, pay books, and general correspondence, looking as if this room had been used as ship's office. Also the coding machine was found here, plugged in and as though it was in actual use when abandoned. The general appearance of this machine being that of a typewriter, the telegraphist pressed the keys and finding results peculiar sent it up the hatch. This W/T office seemed far less complicated than our own sets, was more compact and did not seem to have the usual excess of switches, plug holes, knobs, 'tally's' etc. on the outside.
>
> "Forward of the W/T office was the hydrophone office. This was about the same size as the W/T office and about twice as large as the A/S [ASDIC or sonar] cabinet in *Sealion*, the only [British submarine] I have been out in.
>
> "The hydrophone set was still running and the sensitivity could be increased or decreased by a control knob and the bearing on the gyro dial could be altered.
>
> "Some equipment from the hydrophone office was now unscrewed but on trying to pass it up the hatch by heaving line it was found to be too large to go through. All officers' gear was now searched and several slips of paper, wallets, cameras, etc. were found and sent up."

While *Broadway*'s boat was ferrying books, charts and documents, etc. to *Bulldog*, the wind and sea were rising and the visibility had shut down to 4 miles. On one return trip, Baker-Cresswell sent across sandwiches for his boarders: Balme ate his sitting at Lemp's desk.

The Zeiss binoculars that David Balme used for the rest of his yachting life (Balme)

In parallel with the activity inside the U-boat, which at any moment might blow up or sink under him, Balme calmly prepared *U-110* for towing:

> "During this time I had two hands on the Fxle [forecastle or forward casing] who located the towing bollards which were hollow steel 6" diameter flush with the deck but could be pulled up to a height of about 18" and clipped in position. They had also located wires and hawsers in a porous locker. The only wire was an old and rusty 2" flexible steel wire.
>
> "*Bulldog* now came up my port side and stopped with her stern just off the U-boat's bows and the end of the 2" was sent over to her. I had hoped that this would hold while we got the proper tow secured but as soon as any tension came on it the wire parted. The heavy swell and wind made it impossible for *Bulldog* to remain very close for long as she was drifting to

> leeward faster than the U-boat. However a grass [i.e. coir or floating rope] was now being hauled in but I still only had my original party of 8 men and by the time we had got the end of the wire *Bulldog* had been carried some way off which made the wire heavy to man-handle.
>
> "Two turns were then taken around the bollard but we did not have a shackle to secure the thimble of the wire back on to its own part; the end of the 2" wire was used as a temporary seizing.
>
> "The wire had now got under the U-boat's bows and was being severely chaffed on the sharp edge of the U boat's casing. If this had carried on it would certainly have parted, so I decided to slip the wire. This was probably just as well as *Bulldog* now sighted a periscope and went off on an A/S [anti-submarine] sweep."

Balme and the boarding party were now alone in the Atlantic with no friendly ships in sight. The convoy had made a number of emergency turns that almost carried it out of the range of Schnee in *U-201*, but at last he was able to make the attack that earlier that morning he had agreed with Lemp, sinking the British steamer *Gregalia* and badly damaging the British *Empire Cloud.* While *Amazon* and *Broadway* counter-attacked and began to drop depth charges, nearer at hand a lookout in *Bulldog* thought he saw a periscope and she commenced her own hunt. For Balme:

> "This was indeed a desolate and awful moment. There was I, with my boarding-party, aboard *U-110*, in the middle of the Atlantic, alone with no ships in sight with the wind and sea gradually increasing."

The visibility had decreased too and *Bulldog* would have to find *U-110* again at a spot in the Atlantic by dead reckoning. Dodds and Balme and their parties collected many trophies too: several pairs of Zeiss binoculars; at least one Eumig cine-camera, with which Balme and Dodds filmed the interior; Lemp's Iron Cross; the submarine's visitors' book, and a good many other pieces. One of the cameras was in the radio room:

> "A cine-camera was found in the W/T office and with this I took a few shots of W/T [wireless] and H/D [hydrophone] offices at point blank range but as I afterwards discovered range on camera was set to 25 feet and aperture to f 2.5. I doubt if they will come out at all."

Pollock claimed that it was he who broke open a drawer in Lemp's cabin and took out "sheets of instructions" and packed these and "any little notebooks, or reference books, anything which was portable" into a briefcase. There was no hurry, there was even time for the boarders to ogle the illustrations in a book of "naked ladies" that Pollock found – and was he ribbed about this whenever in later years he met other ratings from *Bulldog.* When Dodds showed Balme the wardroom visitors' book, they could not resist adding their names as the last entries.

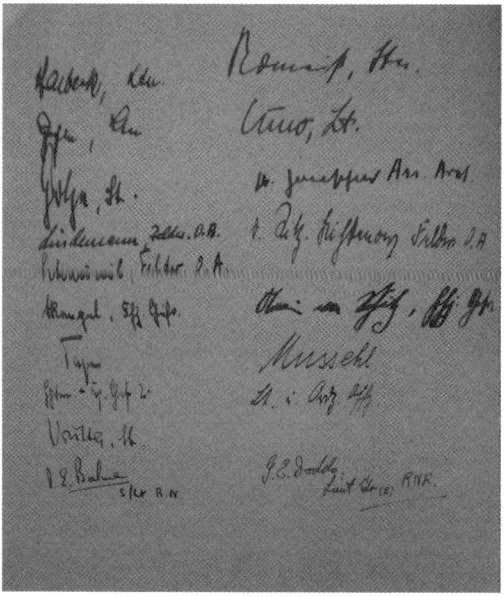

Balme and Dodds signed the their names on the last page of U-110's visitors' book

Balme recalled:

> "I had now been on board about five hours. During this time the U-boat had been going down very slowly by the stern and taken on a list to port as if the port after ballast tank was slowly flooding. It seemed as if all possible material had been recovered so it was decided to batten down and wait for *Bulldog*'s return.

Fortunately, Baker-Cresswell was a superb navigator and *Bulldog* appeared from out of the mist after her U-boat hunt:

> "We were very, very glad to see her, having been all alone in the Atlantic.
>
> "Throughout these hours our escort vessels were attacking U-boats with depth charges and my fear was that their explosions, which felt very close, would set off the detonating charges."
>
> "On Bulldog's return she again came up the port side and with the extra hands and shackle having previously supplied by boat the tow was again successfully secured."

David Balme with Lemp's cap, which he took as a souvenir from U-110 (Balme)

The convoy now was out of sight, and Baker-Cresswell was sure that no ship in the convoy had witnessed the capture of the U-boat. Indeed, from the amount of gunfire they must have heard, he supposed that they imagined the submarine had been sunk. At 16:00 Baker-Cresswell passed the order, 'Batten down and prepare to take on tow'. Balme takes up the story again:

> "This must have been about 16:00. There were no more books or moveable gear we could collect, so I battened down the watertight hatches and we waited. Happily, the *Bulldog* [had] returned and we set about securing a tow. The boat which had been left with us, went over to the *Bulldog* and brought back our Chief Bosun's mate, who was a great help. We eventually managed to secure a tow across."

The logs of the ships involved have not survived into the archives and the precise timeline of what became known as Operation Primrose is hard to establish. Balme's recollection that a boat had been left with him is thus important. This could only have been *Broadway*'s boat, and since *Broadway* and *Bulldog* were on a U-boat hunt between 14:30 and 16:00, this helps to establish that Dodds and his party must have boarded *U-110* after Balme at about 13:00 but before 14:30 when *Broadway* and *Bulldog* charged off into the mist. However, there is a discrepancy where *Aubretia*'s action report says that she picked up thirty-four [German] survivors at 14:30, as elsewhere Baker-Cresswell says that they were picked up before Balme boarded *U-110*. The probable order of events and their times is given in *Annex B The Timeline of Operation Primrose*.

When at last the tow was connected, the U-boat seemed to have some starboard wheel on and it was only with some difficulty that she could be turned to port on to a course for Iceland. When *U-110* was towing nicely at 4 knots, Baker-Cresswell ordered Balme and his crew to rejoin *Bulldog*:

> "The tow held and thus at about 18:30 we evacuated the U-boat and returned to the *Bulldog* after having spent six hours in *U-110*."

Balme finished his official report by writing that "that service revolvers are far too cumbersome and dangerous for boarding and that small police model automatics should be supplied to all boarding officers." He regretted also that in addition to ransacking the wardroom, the crew's quarters should have been more thoroughly searched, but it was his judgement, "that owing to frequent depth charge attacks continuing in the vicinity, considered it safer to keep the watertight doors closed."

He ended his report with a list of his whaler's crew, who had "worked splendidly". They were:

Able Seaman Cyril Dolley
Ordinary Seaman Arnold Hargreaves
Stoker Cyril Lee
Telegraphist Alan Long
Able Seaman Sidney Pearce
Able Seaman Richard Roe
Ordinary Seaman John Trotter
Able Seaman Claude Wileman

Missing from Balme's list was Scotsman William Pollock.

HMS Bulldog's crest

The ship's mascot – with Walter Higgs (c) and George Dodds (Dodds)

Attempting to tow U-110 – HMS Bulldog's distinctive marked funnel can be seen in the foreground (Balme)

When everyone was back on board *Bulldog*, speed was increased to 6 knots and *U-110*, though she had settled slightly more aft, seemed seaworthy enough and surged along at the end of the tow.

> "So we [had] spent six hours in that U-boat, and thus ended an unforgettable day which had far-reaching consequences."

By midnight on 9–10 May the speed of the tow had been worked up from 4 to 7 knots, but they were still some 400 miles from Reykjavik. *Broadway*, which had lost much fuel when she collided with *U-110*, reported she had just sufficient to reach Iceland. Sea conditions worsened during the night and by dawn the wind was blowing hard. The U-boat had settled lower by the stern and was yawing wildly.

Balme recalled:

> "Anyway we went through the first night reasonably and next morning it was still there and we towed it along up to Iceland but, at about 11 o'clock that morning, the seas got up a bit and suddenly the U-boat's bows came right out of the water and she slowly began to sink and we had to cut with an axe the towrope, a great big wire tow rope, and let her go down."

Next day, the Admiralty signalled that the capture of *U-110* was to be referred to as Operation Primrose and that it was to be treated with greatest secrecy, with as few people allowed to know about it as possible. Baker-Cresswell and all the Bulldogs were crushed by the loss of their prize. Baker-Cresswell may even have felt anxious that he had been in dereliction of his duty as escort leader for the safe and timely arrival of the convoy, when he signalled at 11:10 the loss to the Admiralty, 'Primrose has sunk'. He recorded his disappointment in his official report:

> "There were no incidents that night and the submarine seemed to be quite comfortable at the speed of the tow.
>
> "The wind had risen slightly and was S.W. force 4 at 04:00. By 07:00 it had veered to W. by S. and increased to force 6 with a nasty lumpy sea. It was now impossible to hold the course and it was decided to let the submarine head down wind, as she seemed comfortable in this position, and to keep the wire just taught.
>
> "Suddenly at 11:00 the U-boat began to sink by the stern. Very shortly her bow was standing vertically out of the water. She slowly sank and the wire was cut. The prize must have been working slightly in the heavy sea and this may have aggravated any damage caused by depth charges or contact with *Broadway*. Her loss was a bitter blow as it was felt that having survived so many shocks, particularly *Broadway*'s depth charge close to her bow, she should be able to stand the 400 mile tow to Iceland."

Baker-Cresswell's disappointment was shared by all in *Bulldog*, but with hindsight Balme saw the advantages from the point of view of security:

> "We were all very disappointed, but of course, in effect probably the best thing that could have happened because there were so many spies in Iceland, if they'd seen us towing in a U-boat they would have reported it immediately back to Germany. As it was they just saw a routine destroyer coming in to refuel and didn't suspect that anything dramatic had happened."

Bulldog and *Amazon,* carrying the prisoners, reached Iceland late on 10 March, when *Bulldog* refuelled alongside the cruiser HMS *Birmingham*:

> "It was a great triumph and we went alongside one of the big cruisers there, refuelled and amid great excitement with intelligence officers flying out from England, but of course it was about forty-eight hours after we'd captured the U-boat. The prisoners were put into the cruiser alongside, then it was decided, the Admiralty decided, the prisoners should be put on board *Bulldog* who should come back to Scapa Flow, probably I suppose it's about a thousand miles, at full speed. There was a terrific dash to get all the information back to London."

The crews of *Amazon, Aubretia*, *Broadway* and *Bulldog,* as well as the rescued men from the steamer *Esmond*, some 400 men in all, many of whom had witnessed events, were sworn to silence. Balme's report of the boarding, written two days later and headed "Boarding Primrose", might have compromised the meaning of the cover name, but his was not the only potential breach of security.

Knowledge of the boarding of *U-110* was also at risk of compromise from the souvenir hunters. William Pollock, having been soaked, had changed in to a dry uniform that he thought belonged to Lemp. George Dodds, the engineer, kept a photograph album and the visitors' book, which he had found in the U-boat's wardroom,[45] and he and Baker-Cresswell and Balme acquired fine pairs of Zeiss binoculars clearly marked with the German swastika. Dodds kept a camera. Even Jimmy Green, a rating who was at sea for the first time in *Bulldog* and who had seen the boat traffic between the stricken U-boat and his ship but taken no direct part in ransacking the boat, managed to lay his hands on a signal lamp with *U-110* painted on in white, and a 'U-boat jacket made out of some plastic material.'[46]

Balme, a member of the Royal Yacht Squadron, used his binoculars in his various yachts for the rest of his life. He also kept Lemp's uniform cap, which he took from the captain's cabin in the U-boat, a cap that he kept until he presented it to the Imperial War Museum in 2003. Baker-Cresswell kept *U-110*'s chronometer and on the evening of 9 May he used a newly acquired German sextant to take the evening stars, and found it much better than its Admiralty equivalent.

Baker-Cresswell also used his souvenir binoculars in 1943 when he was escort training captain to Admiral Sir Max Horton, Commander-in-Chief Western Approaches, in HMS *Philante*, when someone, surely, must have admired his binoculars and asked him how he came by them!

Baker-Cresswell (c) wearing his pinched Zeiss binoculars: it seems unlikely that no one admired them and asked how he got them. All the other binoculars in this picture are RN-issue 7x50s marked with the broad arrow (Baker-Cresswell).

11

THE PRIZE FROM *U-110*

Later Balme recalled more detail of the inside the U-boat:

> "Here are some of my impressions of the U-boat. She was new and a fine ship both in the strength of the hull, in the fittings and instruments and general interior construction. Absolutely nothing "Ersatz" about her. Excellent A.A. [anti-aircraft] armament abaft the conning tower, consisting of a Bofors and Oerlikon type gun. Deck around the forward gun was wood.
>
> "Spotlessly clean throughout. Wardroom finished off in light varnished woodwork and all cupboards were numbered with corresponding keys to fit. No signs of a safe and there was only one cupboard for which I could not find the key; this cupboard was over the captain's desk so I broke into it and it revealed a medicine chest. In W/T room there were several sets of writing paper and envelopes, well printed and illustrated reading books, cards, dice, and the usual art studios. Bunks were one on top of another both in officer' and crews spaces. An S.R. Equipment [sound recording equipment i.e. broadcast radio] was running all round the boat with very compact S.R.E. receiver (3 feet by 1 foot by 1 foot) in the W/T office with names of about 200 stations written on its dial.
>
> "Plenty of tinned ham, corned beef, cigars, Players cigarettes (German printing on packets) and a plate of shrimps were all found in the W/room [wardroom]. Magnificent galley forward of W/room.

"No signs of voice-pipes but I think loud-speakers and telephones were used, definitely a telephone in the conning tower.

"1 Tommy gun was found in officers' clothes drawer; other L.C.T. with anti-tank type of rifle. Officer gear consisted of very good clothing including well designed anti-weather garments.

"In engine room I noticed a plate of mashed potatoes as if action stations had been sounded suddenly while dinner was being taken from galley to after crew's space. Escape chamber was in C.R. [control room] just abaft the upper hatch (see plate diagram)

Balme was puzzled why no attempt had been made to destroy any books or material:

"Obviously because they thought the U-boat was certain to sink at once, [and] the necessary demolition switches or other devices had been set; this was corroborated by statements from prisoners who had no idea that the U-boat had been boarded."

But, he wrote in capitals:

"WHY WERE BOTH CONNING TOWER HATCHES CLOSED?"

"The most important thing, of course, was the wireless office, and my telegraphist who was in my party went there and took all the settings of the wireless sets, and the rest of the crew, I got them to send all the charts up, up the ladder, it was all quite difficult because you had one arm for the ladder and you only had one arm to take books and charts and things. Anyway we eventually got them up, and then the wireless office, everything was within about 6 feet of each other, it was all so small the inside of a U-boat, the chart table and then the wireless office and I went over to see my telegraphist [Alan Long] who was taking all the settings, making a note of everything, and he said to me: 'There's a funny sort of instrument here, it looks like a typewriter but when you press the keys something comes up on it.'"

Neither Balme nor telegraphist Alan Long knew anything about Enigma, but they were both intrigued by this strange looking typewriter.

> "And we both thought it looked very interesting, probably some sort of decoding machine, so I said: 'Can you unscrew it?'
>
> "And he [Long] had a little set of tools, very well equipped, and he unscrewed all the screws and this thing, about 2 feet by 1 foot, I suppose, was the famous Enigma machine. The Morse code on their Enigma machine would come in from Berlin on to their machine and would be immediately transposed into another code, and by pressing a button you got a different message. This was the famous Enigma coding machine, which we, the Navy, had never managed to capture before. Anyway we unscrewed it and sent it up. Quite difficult, about 2 feet by 1 foot and quite heavy, and one only had one arm for the machine and one arm for going up the ladder. Quite difficult. Anyway we got it up. Got it into one of the boats and back to HMS *Bulldog*.
>
> "This was the first time that the British had ever got a German Enigma machine and it was worth untold gold."

It not was, strictly, the first time that the British had ever got a German Enigma machine. Enigma had been invented in the 1920s, when it was used commercially, and it had only later been adapted by several countries to military use. Starting in 1932, Polish military intelligence had 'broken' German Enigma machines using reverse engineering, mathematics and material supplied by the French.

The Enigma machine consisted of a set of rotors that were driven electrically. Coding was achieving by the setting of the rotors, and each rotor had twenty-six positions, one for each letter of the alphabet. There was a choice of rotors to install (at this stage of the war the German navy used three rotors from a choice of eight). The order of the rotors could be changed, and the initial position for each could be varied. There was also a plug board, and all of this equipment was changed and set differently each day. In addition, each individual message was encrypted using an additional, three-letter key modification. The Poles devised mechanical devices for breaking Enigma ciphers, but as the Germans introduced more complexity to their Enigma machines, decryption became more and more difficult, requiring resources that the Poles did not have.

In 1939 the Poles shared their knowledge with the British and French, and, after the fall of France, Britain exploited this knowledge alone. Through German procedural flaws, operator mistakes, and capture of key tables and hardware, British codebreakers gradually mastered Enigma. At first the intelligence gained from read Enigma and other sources was known as Boniface, but from 1941 onwards it was designated as Ultra. Ultra was particularly important in the Battle of Atlantic because of the way in which the U-boats were operated.

Balme had unwittingly been present when Karl Dönitz had made one of his first essays in wolf pack tactics, when the Hartmann pack had attacked the ships that were being so stoutly defended by Balme's *Ivanhoe* and her sister ships in October 1939. Dönitz's lesson from the Battle of Convoy KJF3 was that he must exercise greater tactical control of his U-boats from his headquarters ashore. Instead of attacking convoys piecemeal, his U-boats were to operate in wolf packs and to co-ordinate their attacks. For this Dönitz relied increasingly on wireless. U-boats were spread out along patrol lines across the path of the convoys, and once one boat sighted smoke or masts or heard propeller noises on her hydrophone, she was to report the convoy to BdU, U-boat headquarters, and to shadow, sending repeated reports of the convoy or a homing beacon. On the surface the U-boats were usually faster than the convoys and they could shadow from ahead. BdU would call up other U-boats so that when an attack developed the escorts would be overwhelmed by packs of half a dozen or more. All this required a great deal of signalling, and if the British, from their Operational Intelligence Centre (OIC) in London, could read BdU's signals, convoys commanders could be warned of an impending attack and be reinforced, and the convoys could be diverted away from concentrations of U-boats.

As well as early, partial access to Enigma, the British had had some success in cracking German codes through a frontal assault on the vast number of coded messages that were picked up at direction-finding stations around the British coast (known as Y-stations), using the famous Bombe machines. However, this took many, many hours and often intercepted messages were not decoded until days after they could have been useful.

During the course of the war the British had also captured some Enigma material, both individual rotors and sometimes settings. Three rotors had been taken from the survivors of *U-33*, sunk on 12 February 1940 in the Firth of Clyde by the minesweeper HMS *Gleaner*. Unspecified documents had been seized from *U-49*, sunk on 15 April 1940 off Norway by the destroyers *Brazen* and *Fearless*. Also, on 26 April 1940 cypher settings had been taken from the armed trawler *Polares*, captured by the destroyer HMS *Griffin*, and when they reached the Government Code and Cipher School (GCCS) at Bletchley Park it had enabled Enigma to be read for a few days in retrospect.[47] The British learned enough to know that there were various key settings, and that 95 per cent of all German naval signals were enciphered in the German 'home' or Heimisch key, which was used in common by most surface ships, U-boats and their supply ships. The 'foreign' key, which was used by German raiders, both warships and armed, disguised enemy merchant ships, was never broken.

Bletchley Park wanted more: it wanted a 'pinch' as such captures were known, and in August 1940 the Naval Intelligence Department had sponsored a Confidential Admiralty Fleet Order (CAFO), an order that was suitably enigmatically worded:

> "It is known that many German Naval Signals are cyphered on a machine. A photograph of a cyphering machine is

reproduced (see CAFO Diagram 242/40) and that used by German Naval units may be of similar appearance.

"Any machine of this type found on board a German man-of-war should be carefully packed and forwarded to the Director of Naval Intelligence, Admiralty, in charge of an officer, by the quickest possible route. It is important that the machine should not be touched or disturbed in any way, except as necessary for its removal and packing."[48]

Plans were also laid for several deliberate pinches. On 4 March 1941 during a commando raid on the Lofoten Islands sufficient new Enigma material was captured from the armed trawler *Krebs* to enable naval Enigma to be read for the whole of February 1941 and at various dates from 10 March. Armed with the knowledge gained, it was also possible to read Enigma by cryptanalytic means for April 1941 for much of May 1941, but with a delay of three to seven days.[49]

Then, when an analysis of traffic showed that the Germans were keeping weather ships on station in the Atlantic and these ships were using Enigma, the Admiralty planned two more pinches. Early in May 1941 the German weather ship *München* was hunted by a British squadron and boarded off Jan Mayen Island by HMS *Somali*. *München*'s crew had time to throw their Enigma machine overboard but other Enigma documents were recovered. (A second pinch of the weather ship *Lauenburg* on 25 June 1941 was even more successful.)

However, the beauty of Balme's pinch inside *U-110* was that it was so complete. The pinch consisted of an Enigma machine, complete with its actual settings for 9 May 1941, a full set of rotors, the 'home waters' settings for April and June (which were duplicated by those pinched from München). Also pinched, from Lemp's cabin, were the special settings used in the German navy for 'officer only' traffic, and the code book used in the U-boat fleet for making the short signal sighting reports – making it possible for the first time for the British to read these two important types of traffic and to reconstruct later editions of them. All that was missing was the settings for the month of May, which were either destroyed during the panic evacuation of *U-110* or, more likely, lost during the transfers of materiel to HMS *Bulldog*.

Balme summarised this:

> "One did need a daily setting to put on it [Enigma] every time so it was only half the battle to have the machine, but we found a month's daily settings in the captain's cabin, so that did us for a month, and it was all sent down to the secret signal school at Bletchley, just north of London. It got there within about 48 hours, first by tugboat to the mainland and then by special car and Royal Marine guard motored the whole 600 miles down to London with it. I think this was the only time we captured an enigma machine. We had the machine but of course we didn't have the daily settings, and this is what Bletchley and all our WRNS now spent their time on, trying to find the daily settings as soon as possible. Sometimes, by incredible mathematicians there, they found it within a day or two and sometimes it would take ten days. It was really not much use for messages then. They were telling the submarines which convoys to attack, [sometimes] they'd already been attacked by the time we had decoded the messages but at any rate a lot of the time we got it in time and saved thousands of ships."

Balme's pinch from *U-110* also included her war diary, at least twenty large-scale charts showing the German navy grid, charts showing the safe routes through German minefields in the North Sea and along the French coast, decoded U-boat signals for the period 15 April to 9 May, administrative correspondence, communications instructions, technical manuals and diagrams for the Type IXB U-boat, and hundreds of mundane items down to the citation for Eichelborn's award of the Iron Cross, but most important of all were the German bigram tables that Bletchley needed to develop its cryptanalytical process known as Banburismus.[50]

> "Anyway we got back to Scapa Flow, the intelligence officers had all come up from the Admiralty, and everything was looked at. I looked after the intelligence officers. A lot of the documents, books of course were pretty wet, they'd been in a small boat coming back, but we got them all dry [and it] was dried and photocopied, everything was photocopied. And then they were put into a drifter and taken over to the mainland, about five miles, and where there was a Royal Marine car and escorts and they all rushed down with the intelligence officer down to Bletchley who were the first people really to know what a valuable catch this had been, the first time that we'd ever captured the German codes.
>
> "We had the codes and all the machines, but of course we didn't have the daily settings, and that was the task of Bletchley to find the daily settings, every day, sometimes this very intelligent team would get the settings somehow within a few hours but more often a few days but sometimes ten or twelve days, which was rather too late to be of any great use. But anyway we did get a lot of good up-to-date intelligence which must have saved thousands of convoys from being attacked by the U-boats, whose positions were broadcast by Berlin in code every day. So once we had the codes, we could break it, sometimes it would take some days to break it, because we had to experiment to find the daily settings."

The war at sea and in particular the Battle of the Atlantic was profoundly changed by the secret capture Balme had made. Bletchley began to read continuously and with little or no delay the wireless traffic in the 'home' or Heimisch settings of German naval Enigma, which were common to most of the German surface navy and to U-boats in the Atlantic and the Mediterranean. The combined effect of these captures was to enable Bletchley to read all German naval signal traffic for June and July, including 'officer-only' signals, concurrently with the intended German recipients. It also gave Bletchley such an insight into the workings of Enigma that by the beginning of August "it had finally established its mastery over the home waters settings, a mastery which enabled it to read the whole of the traffic for the rest of the war except for occasional days in the second half of 1941 with little delay. The maximum delay was 72 hours and the normal delay was much less, often only a few hours."[51]

Balme's pinch saved countless Allied ships and lives, and brought about the end of numerous U-boats and their crews. Ultimately, in the opinion of one naval historian, it led two years later to a German retreat from the North Atlantic, which was a strategic victory as important as the Battle of Midway in the Pacific and the Battle of Stalingrad in Europe.[52]

The armed boarding party rowing to U-110

12

UNTOLD GOLD

The efforts to capture additional, human intelligence began at once. In the brief hours that the prisoners from *U-110* were in *Aubretia*, resourceful officer's cook James O'Brien pretended to be a disaffected Irishman, and chatted to the Germans. *Aubretia* made this report:

> "Prisoner No 1.Wireless Operator, stated that the complement of the submarine was 47. He gave no further information.
>
> "Prisoner No 2. O'Brien spoke as if he did not like the English to encourage the prisoners to speak. This prisoner stated that before the war he had been a journalist on a paper (of which the translated title was Southern Gazette). When the war began he was a driver in a motor transport unit. After the collapse of France he volunteered for submarine service. During a discussion on papers, the theatre, films he said he had seen the film *Mon Ami* in Paris LAST SUNDAY (caps sic). Regarding the war, he said that the German troops were going on from Tobruk to Alexandria to cut the road to India. He further stated that Boulogne had been badly bombed, and had been partially evacuated. As to the attack the prisoner said that we were in contact with another submarine which did not surface! He admitted that he came from *U-110* and that all the prisoners on the fore mess deck were from the same submarine.

"O'Brien also spoke with the 3rd Officer of the submarine; this officer stated that he had stayed in the hotel in Lorient; where the French people in charge of the hotel were anxious for a relative of theirs in England. He was afraid to go to England or Canada because the former was going to be more heavily bombed than ever before during May and the voyage to Canada was dangerous on account of the number of German submarines in their vicinity at the time of the attack. Invasion: he did not think this likely just yet because Hitler on the 5th May had said that Britain was to be bombed first until she was tired of it. The war might end sometime after the end of this month. O'Brien asked him what he had had for lunch, supposing that it would be tinned food. 'Oh no', the officer replied, 'we had fresh food'."

The prisoners were transferred from *Aubretia* to *Amazon* and then to *Bulldog*, where Baker-Cresswell did what he could to gather intelligence from the prisoners:

"I talked a good deal with the four officers captured from *U-110* and had two hours' talk with the 1st Lieutenant, Ober-Leutnant. Hans Joachim Eichelborn [a mistake: Eichelborn was the chief engineer].

"They had a tremendous admiration for their Captain, Capitan Lemp, and were disturbed about his loss. He had evidently impressed on them that big risks must be taken. It was almost impossible to extract any operational details from them but I elicited the following facts.

"They realised that it would have been less risky to have attacked by night. This did not affect their decision. The inference is that they have to wait until other U-boats have been summoned.

"They saw the strength of my ASDIC line but were confident they could get in an attack. They had not seen *Aubretia*.

"They could not understand how we had detected them

as they said they had methods of preventing detection. The inferences that they put great faith in the ruse of getting in a ship's wake. (see E.R.A. Mathews report).

"It is doubtful whether they know much about ASDICs.

"The number of the U-boat is not allowed to be divulged. They were angry that one of the crew had given it away.

"They were confident that the U-boat had sunk before we could reach it, there was not the least suspicion in their minds that we had boarded it. (They were naturally taken below as soon as they were picked up by *Aubretia*).

"They expected that we would have left the convoy before the morning of 9th May, and were surprised that we were still there and wondered if we would still have been with them [in the] evening.

"I had told ERA Mathews what I particularly wanted to find out. He talked some French and [made] friends with war correspondent in the crew. I consider that Mathews played his part extremely well and elicited some valuable information. The war correspondent may well be persuaded to talk further.

"ERA Mathews' report and the report received from *Amazon* are attached."

It is clear from subsequent interrogation that Ecke, the German war correspondent from the Propaganda Kompanie, did indeed 'spill the beans'. Mathews' report read:

"The prisoners were most confident we had no knowledge submarine was in the vicinity until convoy was attacked and surmised we followed wake of torpedo and guessed position. Were quite indignant at the idea they could be heard.

"They said *Seal* [HMS *Seal*: a British submarine captured by the Germans in the Kattegat on 5 May 1940] was submarine training ship at Kiel. When told *Seal* was faster than any German U-boat since she had a speed of 8 knots submerged, they were quite sure German submarines could travel at least

1½ times this speed. When questioned as to exact speed were reticent to talk and said this was specialty of German navy.

"Said they had followed American destroyer [i.e. the four-funnelled lend-lease *Broadway*] for quite a time but would not disclose any definite time but obviously knew convoy had been attacked on previous occasion.

"Apparently they had seen convoy and saw escort proceeding parallel with them. They submerged and fired, and on coming to the surface were depth charged which caused lights to fail. At this moment crew panicked but had lights on again on reaching the surface with partially blown tanks.

"Were most surprised to see destroyers steaming towards them for on last occasion they had been steaming parallel with them and destroyers should have passed on.

"Some report 3 (others 4) submarines were waiting on either side of the convoy and it was dependent on which way convoy turned, which submarine fired.

"When asked if German propaganda had told submarines could not be detected immediately behind destroyers it was obvious such was the case from the talking amongst them as well as an agreement."

When the prisoners reached England, and before they were shipped to Canada to spend the rest of the war in remote camps, they were thoroughly interrogated. The report of this interrogation ran to thirty-seven pages, covering the crew, *U-110*'s previous operations, details of the boat, intelligence about other U-boats, U-boat losses and U-boat bases, tactics, technical details, engineering drawings and photographs.[53] There was also a translation of Lemp's pocket diary, though in the diary he had not recorded any detail about his sinking of *Athenia* on 3 September 1939. Instead. Lemp had duly noted that England and France declared war on Germany but, apparently, nothing occurred during the following week that Lemp thought worthy of notice. Quite apart from the pinch of Enigma, the intelligence gained from the prisoners was coup of the first order.

Meanwhile, Baker-Cresswell was bitterly disappointed to lose his prize. He felt that the weather had cheated him, but the cryptanalytical gains from *U-110* were beyond price – as Balme would say, "worth untold gold."

Bulldog arrived at Hvalford, Iceland, at 01:00 on 11 May, and by 06:30 she had received the prisoners from *Amazon* and sailed for Reykjavik. There, Baker-Cresswell conferred with the flag officer, Iceland, and from there he sailed at 10:30 for Scapa Flow at 25 knots.

Waiting for him on Monday, 12 May was Lieutenant Allon Bacon, a liaison officer between the Admiralty's Operational Intelligence Centre and Bletchley, and a Lieutenant Groves 'from the Intelligence organisation'.[54] From them Baker-Cresswell truly learned the importance of what had been captured.[55] Balme was given the task of assisting Bacon and Groves to sort and dry the papers, which were hung like washing in Baker-Cresswell's cabin. Balme was amused that the Germans had been held prisoner in *Bulldog* while separated only by a thin bulkhead from the captain's cabin, which was festooned with secret papers that had been taken from them. While the prisoners were taken away blindfolded by motor fishing vessel (MFV) at 18:30, Bacon, who had brought only a briefcase with him, was astounded by what he saw. He spent many hours poring over the captured papers, murmuring, "Not this!" and, "This is just what we have been looking for ..." Bacon insisted that everything should be photographed, a task that was not finished until 07:00 on 13 May: he did not want to risk losing anything in transit to London and, as his briefcase was obviously insufficient, eventually all was put into two medium-sized packing cases.

(Later Bacon would lead the team that surprised and captured the German weather ship *Lauenburg* on 28 June 1941, and with the knowledge he had from examining the papers and equipment in *Bulldog*, made a another pinch of cryptographic material that was subsequently described as being of "inestimable valuable".[56])

While Bacon, Groves and Balme were busy in *Bulldog*, Baker-Cresswell took a boat to call on his commander-in-chief, Admiral

Sir Jack Tovey, in the battleship HMS *King George V* and told him and Rear-Admiral, Destroyers, Louis Hamilton, the complete story. He also spoke by telephone to the chief of staff of the commander-in-chief Western Approaches – who told him he was wanted back on escort duty and to sail for Reykjavik as soon as he could get all reports written. Back in *Bulldog*, when Bacon came to say goodbye, he consoled Baker-Cresswell over the loss of U-110: "Never mind about losing the U-boat. From our point of view, it was a good thing, as we can now keep all this quiet. For God's sake never breathe word about this to anyone."[57]

The bigram tables reached Bletchley Park later on 13 May, and at 21:37 that evening, after having been silent for some two days, the teleprinters in the basement of the Citadel in London burst into life as Bletchley began a continuous stream of decrypts. After a briefing from naval intelligence at 23:10 that night the First Sea Lord, Admiral of the Fleet Sir Dudley Pound, sent to Baker-Cresswell at sea a personal signal to say that the petals of his primrose were of rare beauty.

As a direct result of special intelligence gained it became possible to divert convoys around U-boat patrol lines and away from wolf packs. U-boats intercepted and reported only 4 per cent of Atlantic convoys from June to August 1941, compared with 23 per cent during the first five months of the year. In June sixty-one ships of 310,000 tons were sunk by U-boats, but losses fell to twenty-two ships of 94,000 in July and twenty-three ships of 80,000 tons in August.[58]

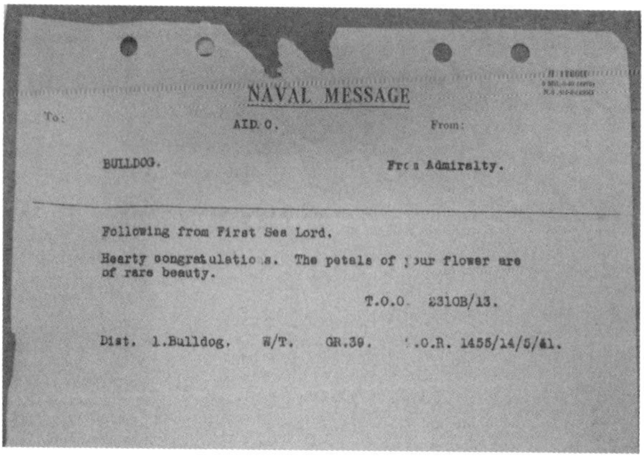
NAVAL MESSAGE

To: AID. O. From:

BULLDOG. From Admiralty.

Following from First Sea Lord.

Hearty congratulations. The petals of your flower are of rare beauty.

T.O.O. 2310B/13.

Dist. 1.Bulldog. W/T. GR.39. T.O.R. 1455/14/5/41.

Signals rarely survived: this one comes from the Baker-Cresswell archive

Patrick Beesly at the Admiralty's Operational Intelligence Centre (OIC) wrote that: 'The tremendous importance of this capture cannot be overemphasized, for U-110's cipher material was valid at least until the end of June … the penetration of [Enigma] just when all our other sources of information were also beginning to produce greatly improved results at last enabled the OIC to function as it has always been hoped it would. It was the equivalent of a major victory in itself.'[59]

13

THE CLOAK OF SECRECY

The cloak of secrecy which was thrown over the pinch from *U-110* was very thorough.

In London the reports on the boarding of *U-110* were read with great interest by the Vice Chief of Naval Staff, who personally directed that the circulation of the file should be limited and it was marked 'Not to pass through any registry'. [60] The war diary of the Commander-in-Chief Western Approaches, which was written up daily, blandly recorded that "9th May … *Bulldog* reports 4 ships sunk in OB318 which was attacked by 2 or 3 U-boats, one of which was possibly sunk. *Bulldog* reports Operation Primrose … *Amazon* had only 5 depth charges left and was returning to Reykjavik to land 41 survivors." There was no other warship mentioned.[61]

The Monthly Anti-Submarine Report for June 1941 (covering the previous month) referred only to "the short life of *U-110*. Such was the end of *U-110*. It was exactly two months since she left Kiel on her maiden voyage; in that time she had only sunk three ships of a total tonnage of 10,085 tons and had seriously damaged a 6,000 ton tanker. Yet she was commanded by an officer of considerable experience and ability, one of the select few who had held commands at the beginning of the war and a man who enjoyed a certain prestige among U-boat captains. He was, it seems, much respected and liked, and was particularly successful in retaining his experienced men. His crew spoke of him as being even-tempered, of great determination and of unshakable calm." This report was not declassified until 1965.[62] There is no clue in the report as to the cause of the panic inside *U-110* and the precipitate haste in which she was abandoned.

Nor did the report of the formal interrogation of the prisoners from *U-110* make any reference to the U-boat having been boarded, searched and ransacked.[63] However, the effect of the pinch was immediate.

Baker-Cresswell in *Bulldog* had sailed from Scapa Flow to rejoin his EG3 at Iceland: they were needed to protect the slow homeward convoy SC31, meeting them at longitude 30° degrees West on 21 May, just when the German battleship *Bismarck* and the heavy cruiser *Prinz Eugen* were about to break out into the Atlantic. Convoy SC31 was just the kind of juicy target that *Bismarck* was hoping to find, and for a while it seemed that the German battleship and Convoy SC31 might be on a collision course. The Royal Navy was stunned to hear that HMS *Hood* had been sunk in the Battle of Denmark Strait on 24 May, and Baker-Cresswell asked if he should leave the convoy to join the hunt for the *Bismarck* but was ordered to stay with his convoy. His pinch of Enigma played little part in the subsequent hunt, and *Bismarck* was brought to bay three days later. However, on 12 June Enigma decrypts did show that the pocket battleship *Lützow* was preparing for sea and gave the Admiralty intelligence about the progress. And on 13 June, after being sighted by an aircraft from Coastal Command, a British striking force of fourteen torpedo bombers attacked *Lützow* and crippled her so severely that she had to return to Germany.[64]

Even more significantly, the British ability to read Enigma led to a slaughter of eleven German ships (tankers, supply ships and a weather ship) that had been deployed into the Atlantic to support *Bismarck* and to extend U-boat operations to areas such as the West African coast. Two of these might paradoxically have been saved by Enigma because the Admiralty, concerned that the sinking of so many ships in so short a time might alert the Germans to the fact that their naval Enigma had been compromised, decided to spare them by deliberately not making use of the intelligence available to it.[65] Luck was running against the Germans because both these stumbled into other, routine Royal Navy patrols: the U-boat supply ship *Gedania* was captured and *Gonzenheim* was scuttled. With refuelling no longer possible, Dönitz had little option but to withdraw his U-boats from operations off West African.

4510 SUPPLEMENT TO THE LONDON GAZETTE, 5 AUGUST, 1941

services when an Italian Convoy and its Escorts were sunk between Sicily and Tripoli:

Bar to the Distinguished Service Order.

Captain Philip John Mack, D.S.O., H.M.S. Jervis.

His Majesty has also been graciously pleased to give orders for the following Appointments to the Distinguished Service Order, and to approve the following Awards:

For enterprise and skill in action against Enemy Submarines:

To be Companions of the Distinguished Service Order:

Commander Addison Joe Baker Cresswell, Royal Navy, H.M.S. Bulldog.
Lieutenant-Commander Vivian Funge Smith, R.N.R., H.M.S. Aubrietia.

The Distinguished Service Cross.

Lieutenant-Commander Thomas Taylor, Royal Navy, H.M.S. Broadway.
Lieutenant-Commander (E) George Edward Dodds, R.N.R., H.M.S. Bulldog.
Sub-Lieutenant David Edward Balme, Royal Navy, H.M.S. Bulldog.

The Distinguished Service Medal.

Chief Stoker Arthur Harry Capelin, P/K.46363, H.M.S. Broadway.
Able Seaman William Samuel Rutledge, P/JX.147777, H.M.S. Aubrietia.
Telegraphist Alan Osborne Long, C/SSX. 25118, H.M.S. Bulldog.

Mention in Despatches.

Lieutenant John Aitken, Royal Navy, H.M.S. Bulldog.
Lieutenant James Olaf Stuart Wilde, Royal Navy, H.M.S. Broadway.
Temporary Sub-Lieutenant Denis Stephen Gore, R.N.V.R., H.M.S. Aubrietia.
Mr. Frederick James Hill, Temporary Acting Warrant Engineer, Royal Navy, H.M.S. Broadway.
Temporary Acting Leading Seaman Cyril Arthur Richard Dolley, P/JX.145165, H.M.S. Bulldog.
Able Seaman Frank Charles Bigg, P/SSX. 16650, H.M.S. Broadway.
Able Seaman Joseph Jakeman, D.S.M., P/J.103411, H.M.S. Aubrietia.
Able Seaman George Edward Lamport, P/JX.141083, H.M.S. Broadway.
Able Seaman Sidney George Pearce, P/J.101154, H.M.S. Bulldog.
Able Seaman Richard Roe, P/JX.173741, H.M.S. Bulldog.
Able Seaman John Trotter, P/JX.191225, H.M.S. Bulldog.
Able Seaman Claude Arthur Wileman, P/JX.214664, H.M.S. Bulldog.
Stoker First Class Cyril George Lee, P/KX.100686, H.M.S. Bulldog.
Ordinary Seaman Arnold Hargreaves, P/JX. 190500, H.M.S. Bulldog.

For coolness, skill and enterprise when an Italian Convoy and its Escorts were sunk between Sicily and Tripoli:

The Distinguished Service Cross.

Commander John William Musgrave Eaton, Royal Navy, H.M.S. Mohawk.
Commander Richard William Ravenhill, Royal Navy, H.M.S. Nubian.
Commander John Anthony William Tothill, Royal Navy, H.M.S. Janus.
Lieutenant-Commander (E) Sydney Vincent Parode Capper, Royal Navy, H.M.S. Janus.
Lieutenant John Fitzroy Duyland Bush, Royal Navy, H.M.S. Nubian.
Lieutenant James Barry Laing, Royal Navy, H.M.S. Jervis.
Lieutenant Lionel Robert Patrick Lawford, Royal Navy, H.M.S. Janus.

The Distinguished Service Medal.

Chief Engine Room Artificer Edwin Jenkins, P/M.38356, H.M.S. Janus.
Engine Room Artificer 3rd Class George Thompson Foy, P/MX.50866, H.M.S. Nubian.
Ordnance Artificer 1st Class George Ernest Hesford, C/M.35343, H.M.S. Jervis.
Petty Officer Thomas Edgar Tribe, P/J.97508, H.M.S. Nubian.
Petty Officer Harry John Whitehorn, P/J. 102361, H.M.S. Mohawk.
Petty Officer Walter Wynne, P/J.94813, H.M.S. Nubian.
Acting Petty Officer Telegraphist James Miller, P/J.110977.
Stoker Petty Officer James Robb, P/KX. 77374, H.M.S. Mohawk.
Stoker Petty Officer William Ernest Sargant, C/KX.79218, H.M.S. Jervis.
Petty Officer Steward Harold James Quick, C/LX.20349, H.M.S. Jervis.
Leading Seaman Robert Charles Wills, P/J. 115277, H.M.S. Janus.
Able Seaman James Robert Arthur, P/JX. 149078, H.M.S. Janus.
Able Seaman Thomas Alfred Reed, P/J. 87611, H.M.S. Mohawk.

Mention in Despatches (Posthumous).

Lieutenant-Commander (E) John Russell de Meza Warren, Royal Navy, H.M.S. Mohawk.

Mention in Despatches.

Engineer Commander James Anthony Ruddy, Royal Navy, H.M.S. Jervis.
Lieutenant Shirley Elliston Jagger, Royal Navy, H.M.S. Janus.
Lieutenant Walter Scott, Royal Navy, H.M.S. Jervis.
Lieutenant Peter John Dixon, R.N.V.R., H.M.S. Mohawk.
Probationary Surgeon Lieutenant Walter Fitzgerald Frazer, M.R.C.S., L.R.C.P., H.M.S. Jervis.
Sub-Lieutenant Kenneth Kirkland Lacey, R.N.V.R., H.M.S. Nubian.
Midshipman Peter Nelson Hopper, R.N.R., H.M.S. Nubian.
Mr. George Douglas Packham, Commissioned Gunner (T), Royal Navy, H.M.S. Jervis.
Chief Petty Officer Ernest Edward Lethbridge, P/J.104458, H.M.S. Mohawk.
Chief Yeoman of Signals Charles Wilfred Harris, C/J.93211, H.M.S. Jervis.
Chief Engine Room Artificer John Henry Hathaway, C/M.34525, H.M.S. Jervis.
Chief Stoker David Chun, P/K.35434, H.M.S. Nubian.
Chief Ordnance Artificer Charles Aubrey Wilson Freeman, P/MX.47568, H.M.S. Nubian.

The honours for Operation Primrose were 'buried' in the London Gazette. Pollock's name was missed off the list.

When the Admiralty's evasive routeing of convoys, informed by the insights it had gained from Enigma/Ultra, made it increasingly difficult for BdU to locate them, Dönitz, did became suspicious 'whether and to what extent the enemy reacted to radio transmissions' and ordered an investigation to be carried out.[66] Various theories were advanced, including coincidence, spying, direction-finding or penetration of the Enigma code system, but the Germans were convinced of the impregnability of their codes and of all the possibilities considered coincidence or spying were held to be the cause. Dönitz himself blamed the increasing effectiveness of British direction-finding and the increased effectiveness of British patrols. When he wrote his memoirs in 1958 he did not appreciate that the British had been reading his prolific signal traffic, and he died in 1980 still not understanding the extent to which his messages had been read.

However, for Balme the rest of 1941 was an anticlimax:

> "And so we settled back into our convoy routine, up to Iceland, then we would leave the convoy and another flotilla would come out and take it on and we'd go in and refuel. When we'd refuelled we'd be ready to bring another convoy back to England. And so it went on. Every three months we had to take the ship in to be boiler-cleaned, because as you can imagine, the saltwater which cooled the boilers got rusted up into all the pipe, and so we'd have ten days boiler cleaning, and then we'd each have five days leave and then to the routine of the convoys."

Balme spent the next three months on convoy duty in *Bulldog* before his next, sudden, reappointment. Not even his certificate of service or 'flimsy' mentioned precisely what he had achieved.

14

OPERATION HARPOON

Balme now suffered an abrupt change of career. Large numbers of RNVR officers had been recruited into the Fleet Air Arm on short service commissions, and the Admiralty, still looking to its long-term officer structure, wanted some officers with permanent commissions, as Balme had, to join the FAA. He recalled:

> "And then suddenly in August, the signal came through to HMS *Bulldog* from the Admiralty saying that Sub-Lieutenant Balme had been selected for an observer's flying course. No one has asked me if I wanted to fly and, of course, it was last thing in the world I wanted to do. I think they chose people who'd done well in their sub-lieutenant's courses. But at any rate my captain got onto the Admiralty, and he knew quite a lot of people there, and said 'This can't be done.' And the Admiralty said 'I'm sorry, we insist. We can't change any of the names because nobody wants to do it, and we've got to have some regular naval officers doing this observers' course.' And, really, came to an end the best time I had in the Navy. HMS *Bulldog* was a small, happy and very efficient ship, and of course on top of all that we'd had this marvellous action in capturing the Enigma machine.
>
> "And so I went down to learn to navigate aircraft. The course, I think, started on 1st September [1941] and finished on about 1st April [1942]. We had to learn a terrific lot of Morse code and signals to communicate with our ship when

we had taken off from the carrier, always by Morse code. Radio-telephony had only just come in and anyway the range was too short, and we would go several hundred miles out from the carriers, looking for U-boats or the enemy ships. We did this course in air navigation up at Arbroath in Scotland. It was quite a pleasant time, good rough shooting there in winter and then in May we, the ten of us, passed the observers' course and waited for our appointments. Mine was to be appointed to a squadron of Albacore, successor to the Swordfish, in the Western Desert a long way from the sea, and to get there I was told I'd have to be the naval liaison officer in a merchant ship in a Malta convoy. These Malta convoys were epic convoys consisting of six or eight ships with an enormous escort of aircraft carriers, battleships and destroyers and we'd try and get them through."

Balme was about to take part in Operation Harpoon, one of two simultaneous British convoys sent to supply Malta, which was under siege by the Germans and Italians. One convoy, Operation Vigorous, was to leave Alexandria in the east, while the other, Operation Harpoon, was to leave from Gibraltar in the west. Each merchant ship in the convoys carried a Royal Navy liaison officer, a team of signalmen and a team of army gunners, and Balme had been selected to command the party in the American-flagged *Chant*, a former Danish ship, of 5,601 tons.[67]

"I arrived at the Admiralty and they said, 'Well, there's no point in trying to take all this luggage with you, you'll probably be sunk, you'll just have to take one suitcase.' So, hastily repacking with my mother there, who'd brought me up in a car, taking most of my luggage back. And then I found myself as naval liaison officer in an American merchant ship, one of the eight merchant ships of a convoy to Malta. Each ship had a similar cargo, a mixed cargo because they didn't expect more than two or three to get there out of the eight which sailed,

> so we had to have a mixed cargo of food, ammunition, fuel, everything you could think of.
>
> "Well, the convoy to Malta started off very quietly and went a long way out into the Atlantic and then into the Straits of Gibraltar. This was the danger point because, of course, the Germans were stationed in Spain which was pro-German and could report back the number of ships going through the Straits of Gibraltar, which they did. We left Gibraltar with a very big escort of two carriers, four battleships, and cruisers."

The convoy left Gibraltar on 12 June 1942, comprising six merchantmen (the British *Troilus*, *Burdwan* and *Orari*, the Dutch *Tanimbar* and the Americans *Chant* and *Kentucky*), which were escorted by the anti-aircraft cruiser HMS *Cairo*, nine destroyers, the fast minelayer HMS *Welshman* and several smaller ships. Distant cover was provided by the battleship HMS *Malaya*, the aircraft carriers HMS *Argus* and *Eagle*, the cruisers HMS *Kenya*, *Charybdis* and *Liverpool*, and a number of destroyers. In the carriers were embarked sixteen Sea Hurricanes, six Fairey Fulmars and eighteen Fairey Swordfish.

> "We had a fairly quiet first day to two but when we got south of Sardinia the enemy aircraft came out and bombed us, but I took over the running of the ship and altered course when I saw the dive-bombers just starting their dive and hoped that we'd avoid the bombs."

No attack on the convoy developed until 14 June, when Italian torpedo bombers sank the freighter the *Tanimbar*, and damaged the cruiser HMS *Liverpool*, which was towed back to Gibraltar by HMS *Antelope*. Before the Strait of Sicily was reached the Hurricanes were flown off to reinforce Malta and the covering force turned back. Meanwhile, HMS *Welshman* pressed on alone to Malta under cover of darkness. The convoy was attacked intermittently during the night by motor torpedo boats operating out of Tunisia, but passed through the strait without loss and was about 70 miles from Malta as dawn broke on 15 June.

There, the promised RAF fighter protection had not arrived when the convoy came under a co-ordinated air and surface attack by Axis aircraft and Italian cruisers and destroyers. Five British destroyers laid a smoke screen and counter-attacked but the destroyers *Bedouin* and *Partridge* were hit and disabled. The tanker *Kentucky* was also hit and set alight, the freighter *Burdwan* was disabled by air attack, and *Chant* came under attack by a skein of German dive bombers. *Chant*'s Danish skipper was paralysed with fright and Balme took command, standing on the open bridge to conn the ship. With an American coxswain at the wheel, Balme looked up to see the dive bombers starting to dive and ordered the wheel to be put hard over as the bombs fell, before ordering another sharp change of course. This went well for several attacks until one bomb hit *Chant*.

> "We did so for about half an hour, one attack after another, but eventually we were hit and of course in a merchant ship you've only got to be hit by one bomb in an old merchant ship for it to collapse and sink. I had a party of four British signalman and eight British army gun crew to man a gun in the stern of the ship, and that's what we were."

She did not blow up, as Balme expected, but a fire broke out and she began to list badly. *Chant* sheered out of line and narrowly missed colliding with *Orari*, another merchant ship in the convoy. Balme was not impressed by *Chant*'s crew, who stole the ship's boats and left him to fight the fire in their ship:

> "All the American crew jumped into the boats and took the boats immediately. We hoped that the ship would survive but there we were left finally, just the dozen or so British soldiers and sailors, and we had to jump into the water. Fortunately it was the Mediterranean and we had the big fleet there and an escort vessel came and picked us up out of the water."

Balme and his sailors were fortunate to be plucked from the water by the minesweeper HMS *Rye*. When the Italian cruisers steamed back to the scene of the battle shortly before noon, *Chant* was on the bottom and her fuel was burning fiercely as it rose to the surface from her ruptured hull on the seabed below. Just two cargo ships limped into Malta with the remnants of the convoy escort on 16 June. In the east, Operation Vigorous was even less successful and the convoy turned back after suffering heavy losses. Balme seemed remarkably unfazed:

> "Funnily enough I was picked up by someone who I had served with before the war in the Mediterranean fleet, was taken into Malta and given a bed for a night or two in what I call the air raid dugouts, which had been drilled out under the city of Valetta in Malta, with two tiers of bunks. We were very safe from the bombing, which went on perpetually in Malta day and night, but nothing could through to those dugouts. But it was only two or three days because everybody was wanted in the war effort and I was wanted in the Western Desert."

Operation Harpoon, or the Battle of Pantelleria as the Italians called it, was one of the few clear victories for the Italian Navy. Balme described the affair and its consequences a little more fully in a letter to his mother in a letter dated 21 June 1942 from the RN Air Station at Dekheila outside Alexandria, after he had been flown overnight in a Hudson to Cairo:

> "Dear Mummy
>
> "I hope you got my cable which I sent off from Cairo at some phenomenal cost. I sent it by the fastest possible method as I thought you might be getting worried with all the Italian claims and the lack of any Admiralty communique (their claims were of course quite ridiculous).
>
> "However I did get sunk on the way out and consequently lost all my gear. As I was travelling fairly light, everything

is claimable except a few things like hairbrushes, clock etc. Fortunately I had all my money on me which has proved most useful and also I had my submarine jacket on at the time. It seemed to keep me afloat all right but I was only in the water about half an hour and it was very warm then. Funnily enough I was picked up by a person called Miller who was in the *Berwick* with me.

"After I was landed, I spent a very interesting two days, living a cave dweller's life. The place we slept in was a long tunnel with two layers of bunks, like in the London tube stations but we were far more crowded. I don't think it is very healthy for a long time like some people have been there, as it gets very damp there and I got bitten from head to foot. It is marvellous the way the place carries on. They managed to supply me with a shirt and shorts.

"I spent a day in Cairo which was very pleasant – I stayed at the Continental Hotel which is frightfully expensive but there was a dear old commander who offered to put me up if I stayed on. I would have done so, except one cannot do anything in Cairo without clothes and can't equip naval people up there. So I came on here and I will tell you more in my next letter. For me, this is evidently quicker than airgraph, so I will send you one of each, per week. For you, regular airgraphs are the thing but airmail postcards are the quickest things if you have anything important to say.

"Hope you can read the pencil all right.

"I can get plenty of money advanced here, while waiting for my claim to go through.

"Love, David"

One can only admire Balme's matter-of-fact reporting, his fortitude and his mother's too during this episode.

15

OPERATIONS OVER THE WESTERN DESERT

The Navy had suffered many losses of ships during the withdrawal from Crete and in operations in the eastern Mediterranean and so, with no carrier available, three squadrons of the Fleet Air Arm's Swordfish and Albacores were put to work in the desert campaign under the operational control of the RAF.

> "I was flown in an RAF transport aircraft, very uncomfortably, lying on the floor to Cairo, and there I was met by the naval officer in charge of the office in Cairo, and I was put up in the best hotel, Shepheard's, for two or three nights, got some uniform, because I had lost all mine, remember, as all my luggage had gone down in the ship I was in, and then I was flown to the naval air base just outside Alexandria."[68]

Shepheard's was the leading hotel in Cairo and one of the most celebrated hotels in the world from the middle of the nineteenth century. Originally called the Hotel des Anglais, it was built in the 1840s, and was renamed in the 1860s after its owner Samuel Shepheard (1816–66). Shepheard's was famed for its grandeur and opulence, although a frequent complaint was that its cuisine left much to be desired. In the First World War, the hotel served as British Headquarters in the Near East. It is likely that Balme stayed here, rather than at its main rival, the Continental Hotel on Opera Square, as he had told his mother in his letter home, because in the Second World War Shepheard's had become a British officers' mess.

The Fleet Air Arm's base was called HMS *Grebe*, at Dekheila, an airfield just on the outskirts of Alexandria, on a narrow strip of land between Lake Maryut and the Mediterranean.

> "There was no respite, I was told that the squadron that I was joining was out in the desert, and we were in full retreat, and they flew me up to join a squadron of Albacores, which were a sort of glorified Swordfish. It wasn't a very nice feeling for someone who'd never really been at a shore station, an air station in the middle of war. The army was in full retreat and alongside our airfield was a single track road and all the personnel carriers and tanks were streaming past and we in our aircraft waited until we heard the gunfire ahead of us and then we took off, tried to bomb the enemy and then flew back to Alexandria."

A Fairey Albacore of 826 Naval Air Squadron (Balme)

Balme was flown up to Sidi Barrani to join 826 Naval Air Squadron. The squadron flew the Fairey Albacore, torpedo-spotter-reconnaissance biplanes and successors to the famous Fairey Swordfish or 'Stringbag'.

From primitive, advanced airstrips in the Western Desert they now flew in support of the 8th Army and, following the fortunes of the 8th Army as it advanced and retreated, the squadron moved up and down the Egyptian and Libyan coasts. Balme recalled that once in the ebb and flow of desert warfare, his aircraft took off eastwards from a small airstrip as he heard the rumble German tanks advancing from the west. In spite of this peripatetic existence the aircraft were kept at a high level of serviceability, higher in fact than any other squadron in the desert. His main recollection during this "rather bizarre period" was "the sight of the army in full retreat, mile after mile of lorries heading back towards the Suez Canal."

> "While in the desert we had one very interesting trip. The distances in the desert are really quite big and no RAF aircraft could go from Cairo to the enemy bases along the North African coast, the distances were too great, so the 12 Swordfish (sic – he means Albacores) of our squadron were sent into the desert behind the enemy lines, where we landed on an old airstrip and we had fuel carriers which refuelled us, all by hand, cans of petrol which we had to pour in, and also the refuelling aircraft carried Royal Marines, who defended the place where we had landed. And we took off to go to Tobruk to try and sink a convoy, a very important German convoy, which was coming from Italy to Tobruk: we did find the convoy, though whether we did any damage or not I don't know, but we dropped our bombs on them, but it was a long trip back to Alexandria, as you can image, it must have taken us about 6 or 8 hours, about as long as you can in one of those old Swordfish (sic) aircraft."

This was the enterprising yet risky Operation Chocolate on 9 July 1942, which Balme, as senior observer, helped to plan. Nine aircraft (one turned back with engine trouble: all were Albacores) flew up close to the frontline at Mersa Matruh and from there to a remote desert airstrip on salt flats south of Sollum and some 70 miles behind enemy lines. There they rendezvoused with five RAF Bombay transports bringing fuel, stores and maintenance personnel, and army commandos to provide ground protection, and they were refuelled before flying a further 180 miles deep into enemy airspace to attack at night a convoy entering Tobruk. The total flying time on this daringly conceived and brilliantly executed mission, there and back, was some 9 hours 45 minutes, and all aircraft returned without loss.[69]

David in the flying jacket that a grandson has inherited for motorcycling (Balme)

The Fleet Air Arm's Operation Chocolate and Balme's role in it is nowadays almost forgotten, but its success was noted by the RAF, who a few months later emulated the operation. For three days in November 1942, when it was the Axis troops' turn to retreat westwards along the coast road after the Battle of El Alamein, they were attacked by two squadron of Hurricanes that had been flown forward to a landing ground base deep in the desert. This second Operation Chocolate, the mounting of a series of offensive strikes by a whole wing of aircraft from an unprotected base scores of miles behind the enemy's forward positions, was described by the RAF – always better at singing its own praises – as "unparalleled in the history of aerial warfare", and despite the RAF losing a Hudson and seven of its thirty Hurricanes the operation was acclaimed as "an extremely bold and successful operation, one carried out in the very best traditions of the Royal Air Force".[70]

On another occasion, a reconnaissance flight by 826 NAS was the first to spot the mass movement of transport and tanks that heralded Rommel's final bid to break through the British positions at El Alamein. A typical entry in a squadron flying logbook reads, "Bombed and machine-gunned tanks and m/t [motor transport] in El Alamein area, Good results. Six tanks reported burnt out by our land forces next day." Occasionally this was varied with minelaying or with spotting for night coastal bombardments by the Royal Navy.

> "And then Montgomery came out [13 August 1942] and he stopped the army at El Alamein. He was the first person to really achieve anything in that dreadful campaign, where we always seemed to be retreating until Montgomery arrived."

Balme's squadron now stayed at Dekheila until after the Second Battle of El Alamein. The morale of British forces was not good and everybody expected to be pushed back across the Canal. Balme was clear:

> "That this did not happen was entirely due to the most fortunate arrival of General Montgomery, who ordered the retreat to stop at El Alamein and said that the army would fight and die there ... and for the next few months Montgomery worked tirelessly to restore morale while reinforcements arrived round the Cape from Britain. Montgomery and Air Marshal Tedder visited all units, including the naval air squadrons. Never was co-operation between the services better."

Balme, as senior observer, planned – and took part in – frequent attacks on German and Italian targets, including aerodromes, vehicle parks, and harbours.

> "As our naval aircraft were so slow, with a top speed of only 90 knots, we operated at night. Basically we were torpedo bomber squadrons and in the hangar at Dekheila there were all our torpedoes under the careful eye of our torpedo officer Morgan-Giles (later to become a famous admiral and MP). As we had nothing to torpedo we carried bombs and were used as dive bombers against German tanks and transport. However, the opposing armies having settled down at Alamein in lines quite close to each other, it was decided to begin round the clock bombing of the Afrika Korps. The difficulty was seeing at night where the lines separated. Navigating over the desert had no landmarks such as rivers or hills or villages but was more like navigating over the sea. The Army, having been bombed at night by the RAF by mistake, said that in future night bombing was only to take place if the Navy did the flame dropping over German lines. Thus began the first pathfinding operations, a system which was later used for all bombing of Germany, etc."

Having successfully providing night illumination flares for the 7th Cruiser Squadron in July 1943, 826 began similar operations for the 8th Army and the Desert Air Force, and Balme was at the forefront of this early development of pathfinder operations.

> "This is when the ingenuity of our torpedo officer, Morgan-Giles, really saved the cause. He invented and had constructed eclectically controlled flare racks to fit under the wings of our Swordfish and Albacores. I think we carried about 20 flares on each aircraft. Our job was to circle over the German lines at about 8,000 feet dropping a flare every few minutes and the RAF Wellington bombers came in underneath us and bombed the illuminated German transport and tanks. Each Swordfish or Albacore spent about 20 minutes dropping flares and this went on all night so one aircraft took off from Alexandria every 20 minutes from dusk until dawn.

"We flew over Aboukir Bay, where Nelson fought his famous Battle of the Nile, and as we went out we did an antiquated but accurate method of determining the direction and strength of the wind. We dropped a smoke flare into the sea and with a stop watch and by steering steady courses we could work out the wind. To the north of the Alamein line there was a prominent point of land from where we took departure. The Army then laid out an illuminated letter with burning oil drums at a predetermined position each night. We knew exactly where we were so took a departure for the German lines where we circled for 20 minutes dropping flares so the whole place was as bright as daylight. The worst moments were when we were caught in the enemy searchlights and they opened fire with heavy and light anti-aircraft guns, the latter looking like a firework display. After the war it took me some five years or so before I could enjoy again a firework display at Henley or Cowes. Our aircraft were so slow that the Germans could not believe it and by turning tightly towards the beam of a searchlight one could usually get away from them.

"At the end of 20 minutes of pathfinding we did a dive-bombing attack with the four bombs which we carried. As we went down almost vertically our 90 knots on the flat increased to some tremendous speed, the whole aircraft shook, things fell out of the open cockpit and it was a great relief when the bombs went and we were on our way back to Alexandria. I wonder how much actual damage either the Wellingtons or ourselves really did but it kept the Germans awake all night for weeks on end before the Army attacked and it must have worn down their morale badly."

It all sounds simple but, there were, of course, losses and it was, Balme said: "The most terrifying time of the whole war for me."

"We used to lose an aircraft and its crew every night – fortunately, I was alright, but eventually after about four weeks of this , when we were over the German lines, our engine seemed to fail, which was an awful moment. So I had to tell, we had a discussion with the pilot, we've got to land so we'll try and find a good beach, because although the desert was fairly flat, there were lots of mounds and rocks, so the beach was the safest place to land, a good sandy beach. So eventually we found a sandy beach behind the British lines and we landed. We did turn upside down as we landed, but that was alright, we were going very slowly by then. Some soldiers dashed out after us, and fortunately they were Egyptian soldiers working under the British, so they sent a message back to our airfield in Alexandria and in about five hours' time they got a truck to us and took us back home.

"And so the night of the Battle of El Alamein eventually came [23 October 1942] and there below us as we continued our flare-dropping the fantastic artillery bombardment took place, the first set piece battle of the war. The continued bombing of the Germans by night went on as we advanced across the desert.

"Well, anyway at El Alamein the British won a great victory there and started an advance, and we all advanced, we with our 12 aircraft didn't dash off immediately, we had to wait till they got to a good position. When they got a place called Benghazi in Tripoli, we moved up and got all our aircraft to this airfield, which was fairly near the German lines."

Meanwhile, living conditions for Balme varied:

"We settled in at Benghazi [where] we made a sort of home in dugouts, old ammunition dumps which the Germans had built, quite comfortable really and very safe, and eventually we moved into villas in the town. One thing I can remember about these villas is that they were all made of marble, and the floors were so slippery, they seemed one of the most dangerous things of the war.

"With our caravan of ground crews with engine spares, ammunition, bombs, etc. we also had our Maltese cooks and stewards who had come ashore with us from our aircraft carrier. We were desperately hungry in the desert and I expect it was because our Maltese stewards did not really know the drill for drawing sufficient rations from the Army quartermaster stores. However, regardless of where we were, our cooks insisted on giving the officers a five-course dinner because this is what they had been taught in their cookery school in Malta. Thus, soup looked like the washing up water, fish was one sardine, joint was a bit of bully beef on a ship's biscuit with one tinned potato, sweet was a prune or tinned apricot, and finally the piece de resistance and the best part of the meal was the savoury, which was a spoonful of scotch woodcock made of dried egg and with the toast the size of a half crown coin. On this diet and with the bracing desert air one felt really hungry".

Balme now succumbed to a common complaint in the desert:

"While I was in the desert, I suddenly caught a very nasty disease called sandfly-fever, which is just a fly in the desert which bites you and gives you a very nasty fever. I was taken into hospital in Alexandria and had a terrible headache for 4 or 5 days, which seemed to be awful, but while I was lying in bed there, recovering, suddenly, there were always stretchers being brought in of people who had had accidents or aircraft crashes but one of the people brought in on a stretcher one day happened to be my pilot. He had crashed into the sea during a dive-bombing exercise and his observer, who had taken my place while I was in hospital, was killed. I suppose that this is the greatest miracle that ever happened to me. If I hadn't caught sandfly-fever, I wouldn't be here today. Anyway, we got good food."

When he had recovered, Balme rejoined his squadron near Tripoli and returned to dropping flares every night on the German lines.

> "Meanwhile, the British had landed in Algiers, so we had a pincer movement on the Germans. I think it was the 1st Army which landed in Algiers and they advanced towards us, and we advanced towards them and, of course, eventually the Germans surrendered after a few months."[71]

Assessing these operations by the Fleet Air Arm from its land bases in the desert, the Air Officer Commanding-in-Chief, Air Chief Marshal Sir Arthur Tedder, reckoned they were "one of the decisive factors in holding Rommel's assaults".[72]

Balme continues:

> "With the Army advancing rapidly to Tripoli there was not so much need for us, so it was decided to fly our 12 Albacores over to Malta, about 150 miles, and there we left them to be used as replacements for the squadron based there ... I always thought flying those Albacores hazardous, uncomfortable, and very frightening ... I never liked the flying but we had some very interesting times with a great crowd of people ... However, I was sitting in the sun one day up in the Western Desert when suddenly I read an Admiralty Fleet Order requesting RN officers to volunteer immediately for a new branch called Fighter Direction. This seemed just the thing so it was only a few weeks before I found myself flying down through Africa in an RAF aircraft."

Messing in the desert – a page from Balme's scrapbook 18

16

FIGHTER DIRECTION OFFICER

With the rapid expansion of the Fleet Air Arm and the Admiralty's successful employment of a new class of ships, the escort carrier, and the deployment at sea of radar there was an urgent need for a new specialisation of officer, the fighter direction officer. The Fleet carriers were nearly 30,000 tons, had 700 feet long armoured flight decks and carried more than forty aircraft, while the escort carrier, called a 'jeep' carrier or 'Woolworth' carrier by the British, were, as the nickname suggests, cheap and quick to build. They were half the length and one-third the displacement of the larger fleet carriers. They were also slower, less well-armed, unarmoured and carried fewer aircraft, typically in mixed squadrons of fighters, torpedo bombers and anti-submarine aircraft. More than forty escort carriers were built, and they proved particularly successful in convoy escort duties and in providing air cover during Allied landings in the Mediterranean. Typically, the Admiralty did not want its new breed of direction officers to all be RNVR officers, who would disappear after the war's end, and called for volunteers from its corps of regular officers. Balme found himself in the forefront of this innovation in naval warfare.

> "I was sitting in a deckchair when another officer, another who disliked this flying business ... We both thought that this would be a really good thing and immediately put our names in, and after it had gone through various processes

at the Admiralty, it was done very quickly, it took only 2 or 3 weeks, we were selected for fighter-direction training and to make our way back to England. Somewhat easier said than done, but fortunately with great efficiency someone organised for us to fly in stages right down to the equator in the Belgian Congo, stopping every eight hours to refuel and then up to Nigeria, and there we waited for a long-range aircraft to take us back to England. The first aircraft took us to Lisbon in Portugal, which was beautiful, and there we put up in a hotel, in plain clothes. Next door we heard German officers talking to each other, a rather funny feeling. At any rate, we took off in a day or two and flew over the Bay of Biscay back to England.

"This was quite a risky route and a famous film star called Leslie Howard was shot down and killed trying to do the same trip. When Leslie Howard was shot down the Germans thought they were targeting and attacking a plane carrying Churchill, who'd actually just left a few days earlier, so Leslie Howard was killed but Churchill survived, which was extremely lucky for us all.

"And so started a completely different part of my naval life. I did a three-month fighter-direction course, which was really interesting and delightful in the country down at Yeovilton, where the Navy had taken over the Sparkford Inn, a lovely little pub, and about fifteen of us there, and were taken in by bus to do this course every day. Well, in three months you couldn't learn a lot and we had to improvise and really teach the fleet the little we knew about fighter-direction ... It was a very new department, we had to improvise as we went along with the radar and the fighters. The great thing was to have good communications; this all depended on your radio mechanics on the ground to see that the sets really worked, and mine seemed to work well and had quite a lot of success against the enemy aircraft."

Rather than being sent to an escort carrier, Balme was chosen to go a battlecruiser. It was a logical decision because the bigger ship would be fitted with better radars, and would, presumably, operate in a fleet or squadron that included fleet or escort carriers.

17

CHURCHILL'S PRIVATE YACHT

Balme joined the battlecruiser HMS *Renown* on 26 May 1943, where his initial duties had little to do with fighter direction:

> "But the important things that happened to me in *Renown* that I shall never forget is that as we were a very fast and very comfortable ship, we were detailed to take the Prime Minister, Winston Churchill, and all his entourage to several of his conferences. One in Cairo, so we went through the Mediterranean, which was all in our hands, and another one in Newfoundland, so we went across the Atlantic."

HMS *Renown* was the first of a class of two 26,500-ton battlecruisers and was built in Glasgow. She was completed in September 1916 and served with the Grand Fleet in the North Sea during the remaining two years of the First World War. After a refit in 1920–21, she carried HRH the Prince of Wales on a voyage to Australia and America. During 1923–26 she was extensively refitted to increase her armoured protection against shells and torpedoes. Then, after a further decade of service, *Renown* was again reconstructed, greatly changing her appearance and giving her a modern anti-aircraft gun battery and up-to-date gunfire control. This work was completed in September 1939, just after the outbreak of the Second World War.

Renown's high speed made her a valuable asset during the war, and Balme had already been at sea, in *Berwick*, with *Renown* at the inconclusive Battle of Cape Spartivento. *Renown* bombarded Genoa on

9 February 1941 with little effect, and after the sinking of the battleship *Bismarck* in May, *Renown* led the force that ran down the German supply ship *Gonzenheim*, which had been intended to resupply *Bismarck*, and she was sunk on 4 June by the cruiser *Neptune* – an event made possible by Balme's capture of the Enigma. Later in 1941 *Renown* was fitted with a comprehensive suite of surface search and air warning radars: it was these radars that gave Balme his role in *Renown* as fighter direction officer. In December 1941 she had taken Churchill to the first meeting of the leaders of Britain and the United States in Washington, codenamed Arcadia, and in 1942 and early 1943 *Renown* was busy on Arctic, Atlantic and Mediterranean convoys. In acknowledgment of the changing nature of the threat, she was gradually fitted with increasing numbers of 20-millimetre Oerlikon anti-aircraft guns in twin and single mounts – eventually she carried seventy-two of these guns.

On 5 August 1943 Churchill had sailed from the Clyde in the Cunard liner *Queen Mary* for the Quebec conference, codenamed Quadrant, a highly secret, top level meeting of British, Canadian and United States governments. Quadrant gave priority to Operations Neptune and Overlord, the landings in Normandy, over the campaign in the Mediterranean, set up a new theatre command in Southeast Asia (SACSEA) with Admiral Lord Louis Mountbatten as supreme commander, and at Quadrant it was also agreed to help the Chinese war effort. After the conference Churchill remained in North America during the negotiations in Italy with the government of Marshal Badoglio over the terms of the Italian armistice.

Renown was sent to bring Churchill and his party home from the USA. She sailed from Scapa Flow on 24 August, and after a stormy passage arrived at Halifax on 29 August. On 14 September *Renown*, with the Prime Minister, members of his family, his advisers and their staff, including a large number of WRNS cipher officers, embarked and she sailed for the Clyde, where she arrived on 19 September.

> "This was a fascinating time because Churchill continued to conduct the war while he was on board, and we and all the

officers were allowed to go into the war room to see his maps of the world and where we were operating. I remember so clearly how Churchill really managed the war himself. There was one evening and he had all his generals and admirals around him and a big map of the Greek islands, the Mediterranean. And this was a rather a disastrous campaign, we were trying to hold on to the Greek islands against a German invasion, and we were gradually being pushed out because the Germans were so strong in the air, and I remember Churchill looking at the map with his cigar one evening and he pointed his cigar at one little island, whose name I can't quite remember now, and said, 'We must evacuate this island, we can't hold it any longer against the Germans, and we'll move down to this island, 50 miles away, and make a stronghold on that island.' It was amazing to see how Churchill really did organise things and gave commands."

Mr and Mrs Churchill greet visitors to HMS Renown (Balme)

Balme added some personal observations about Churchill:

"He'd never drink tea or coffee in a ship because once, some years ago, he'd had a slight taste of diesel in the water, and he'd never forgotten the taste of diesel in the water of his tea. So, he only drank brandy and other spirits, so at breakfast he'd have a brandy and his cigar, with his nightcap on, and he'd take down a signal from the Admiralty, and look at it and grunt. He didn't want to talk about it but he just hoisted it all in. He'd only just be getting up and I remember seeing him lying in his bed after breakfast in his bunk and he had a nightcap on, a most extraordinary thing for a man to have a nightcap on, and a cigar, of course, in his mouth. I would take a message in to him which had come down from the Admiralty, and he'd grunt.

"And, of course, it was the first time and the only time that we had women on board. Quite apart from his family, Mary Churchill – who had her 21st birthday on board with him – and his wife of course, we also had WRNS officers doing all the cipher work, and they were guarded by the Royal Marines at night so nobody could get to their cabins, but it was a fascinating time.

"I remember seeing the family, the Churchill family, walking up and down on the deck as we went through big seas on the Atlantic crossing."

Mary Churchill cuts her 21st birthday cake on board HMS Renown (Balme)

Balme wrote home to his mother:

"HMS *Renown*, 25th Sept 1943

"Here is a full account of our trip over to Canada and back which since its publication in the press, we are now allowed to say anything about. The day before we sailed for Canada, there was obviously something in the air as a number of extra stewards arrived including an elderly Chief Petty Officer Steward who is 'keeper of the Royal Yacht' and who always organises food for important people in warships.

"As soon as we got to sea, we began preparing for the party – carpenters doing their best to turn the ship into a passenger liner: canvas alley ways rigged so that one could get to the bridge entirely under cover, telephones connected in all direction, extra floodlighting for the 'map rooms', canvas screens put around the ladies' bathrooms etc. The best bed in the ship was obtained for Mr Churchill and was tested by the Chief Steward lying on it and seeing if the vibration was too much. The Chief Steward was a typical man Jeeves, accustomed only to serve the very highest and always talked in a hushed whisper in a very dramatic voice, We had a meeting at which this character told us of the whims and wishes of Mr Churchill which was the funniest things I have heard for a long time – that in some warships, Mr Churchill had not liked the taste of the drinking water so he used to have a bottle of white wine for breakfast fortunately our water turned out to be alright – just as well as we only had 2 bottles of white wine on board. Also that he must have ice in large quantities with everything. If he rang a bell he expected it to be answered at once and he sometimes liked a glass of soda water when he woke up in the middle of the night and that he always stuck plasticine in his ears when he went to sleep so that he did not hear any noise.

"We went through a hurricane on the way over there, but it did not affect this enormous ship unduly. In fact, I find it very comfortable at sea and peaceful as I do not have a lot of work to do. We went to Halifax and spent over a fortnight there as the Prime Minister prolonged his stay there, waiting for the fall of Italy. It was just like a hot English summer there and we had great fun.

"The first detachment to arrive were twelve Wren officers and Sir Dudley Pound[73] with his staff. Various unfortunate people were turned out of their cabins and all the girls were given a cabin each. They all loved their trip and made the ship look just like a liner. Old Dudley Pound looked very old and decrepit and appeared once throughout the trip – I see he has now gone to hospital so it looks as if he will die soon. They began fixing up a mass of maps and stuck pins and flags onto them; we were allowed to visit this place, called the War Room, and it was very interesting, seeing the latest movements – one hears pretty well the same scene only about 24 hours later on the wireless.

"The main party of VIPs as they are called (Very Important Persons) arrived about three days later in a special train. They consisted of the Churchill family, General Ismay,[74] Brendan Bracken and various male and female private secretaries, valets etc.

"Churchill was wearing his famous yachting get-up [actually the uniform of a member of the Board of Admiralty] and a large cigar – all his cigars which he seemed to smoke continuously, are especially big ones about an inch in diameter. He was in very good spirits and was up on the bridge as we left harbour. They made a big hit in the ship – Mrs Churchill and Mary got about a lot and talked to the sailors in the mess decks; Mrs Churchill has strained her wrist fishing so bad her arm was in a sling all the time.

"Mary is most attractive and most energetic as she clambered into every hole in the ship and even went up the mast to our crow's nest. She had her twenty first birthday on board the second day out; the ship's cook made a magnificent cake which was lit by 21 electric candles; in the evening she gave a cocktail party in the wardroom which was financially satisfactory to all parties concerned as the mess bill is paid by the Admiralty.

"Mr and Mrs Churchill came in the wardroom on the last evening at sea. She is very charming and very talkative. He was writing his speech for Parliament on the voyage and you could see that his mind was on it all the time as the remarks he made on conversation afterwards turned out to be quotations from his speech. He was very insistent about all satellites and neutrals working their passage to the peace conference and said that this also applied to Mr de Valera[75] although he didn't realise it; but I don't think he said this bit in Parliament. I expect you have seen pictures of Churchill in his ear pads watching a shoot which he specially asked to see. He has a personal photographer who goes everywhere with him, dresses as an Army captain and who takes snaps quietly without being seen. It was a good thing he had him with the party, as otherwise there would not have been many photos taken as I was meant to be in charge of the ship's press party and I was saddled with a half-wit; a sailor who had been at Hollywood and his results were appalling. I hope he was more successful with the ship's cine camera but we have not seen those results yet as we sent them straight to the Ministry of Information for newsreels if they were good enough.

"Brendan Bracken[76] is a very odd man – he came fairly low in the list of VIPs so he was not given all the attention he probably gets when he is at work and I think he was a little hurt that not more notice was taken of him. I think he is a good person to be Minster of Information. He stands no nonsense from any critics; when they were in the States, the Hearst press made a very damaging attack on Churchill and Brendan Bracken saw the author and told him he was an enemy to civilisation and then threw him out without answering his questions.

"General Ismay is a very pleasant person – he has been at his job under some different titles for 8 years ever since the Abyssinian War and probably knows more about the war than anyone.

"The weather coming back was fairly good with a following sea which was just as well as I expect a good many of the girls would have been sick.

"The whole party were evidently more comfortable than even before and so they ought to have been considering all the things which were arranged – a bit of deck above the quarterdeck was even reserved as the Royal promenade deck with canvas all around the sides so the women's skirts were not blown up! Structural alterations were carried out in the ship's cinema so that 6 VIPS could sit in raised armchairs – Churchill always brings his own pre-released films with him; they were not especially good ones this time. Some of them were "Claudia",[77] "Winter Time"[78] with Sonya Henie and Gracie Fields' new film.[79]

"Churchill works very long hours and several times gets up in the middle of the night to see signals and the maps. Communiqués from General Alexander arrived at all times of the day.

"We arrived home on Sunday and before they left he made a speech on the quarterdeck which was very good and delivered very quietly into a microphone and without any notes. Immediately afterwards we had a short service there and the two hymns were specially chosen by Churchill – the first one was about 'for those in peril on the sea' but I have forgotten the proper name,[80] and the other was Onward, Christian Soldiers! Which he sang with great vigour.

"I will send you some photos of the trip when they arrive from the MoI [Ministry of Information]. Could you send this round all the family in turn – Richard and Christian will be able to see it at home and if you could then send it to Maurice, Olive [a sister], Phiggie [a favourite aunt] and anyone else who would like to read it.

"Yours, David"

On 12 November 1943 *Renown* sailed from Plymouth with the Prime Minster accompanied by the American Ambassador, John Gilbert Winant, for Gibraltar, where Churchill was to have taken a plane to Cairo. No plane was available and the journey continued in *Renown* via Malta to Alexandria, steaming at 30 knots and hugging the coat of North Africa where possible: at Malta on 17 November Churchill briefly fell ill. Once in Egypt, Churchill, President Roosevelt and Generalissimo Chiang Kai-shek met at the Sextant conference between 23 and 26 November.

Balme had some work to do as fighter direction officer:

> "These were primitive days of fighter direction and as always depended on good communications between ship and fighters, and this was still unreliable.
>
> "The fighter cover was provided by a cosmopolitan collections of squadrons – Greek, Czech, Polish – so even if we could hear each other, the language was not very easy. Radiotelephony was in its infancy and very unreliable – our own r/t set was about 6 feet tall by 6 feet wide, full of valves and nobody really seemed to understand it, so more often than not I was not in touch with the fighter escort. Churchill always came with his Chiefs of Staff and the First Sea Lord had two very young captains on his staff. From time to time our radar picked up unidentified aircraft and these two staff officers kept on popping into my operations room asking if everything was under control. It would have been no help to anyone to tell them that we were not in control with our fighter escort and the situation was completely out of control! Fortunately it was the days when all this was black magic and my plotters and myself were the only people who understood what went on in this operations room so I just told them that all was well and there was nothing to worry about.
>
> "When we arrived at Malta I managed to get a very good

> wireless warrant officer to spend all night repairing the r/t set. For the second half of the voyage to Alexandria the set worked from time to time and most fortuitously it worked very well on the final 100 miles, when our fighter escort was under the command of Max Aitken,[81] who was a boyfriend of Sarah Churchill who was on board for the voyage. She came into my operations room and had a successful chat with Max Aitken on the r/t. Thus, happily, Churchill and his staff went ashore in the blissful ignorance that [they] had been successfully escorted by fighters from Gibraltar to Alexandria."

Churchill and Roosevelt then travelled on to Tehran to meet Stalin at the end of November, and returned to Cairo to meet Mustafa İsmet İnönü, the president of Turkey between 4 and 6 December. Balme's oral memoirs concludes this episode:

> "And so we took Churchill back to Alexandria, and he went on to two conferences, one in Cairo and one in Russia, Potsdam, I think, or somewhere. The four countries discussed what they would next do and, of course, we were being urged all the time to open up the second front in France."

By 2 December *Renown* was back in Rosyth: Churchill, after a convalescence in Marrakesh, returned home in the battleship HMS *King George V* on 18 January 1944.[82]

18

WAR AGAINST JAPAN

"And so *Renown* returned to England and it was getting on for November, December 1943 and we had been – it was the time when the Cabinet decided it was the moment to open up another front in the Far East. Japan had come into the war against us and driven us pretty well out of Burma. We were pretty much on the Burma–India border and Churchill said we're going to drive the Japanese out of Burma and down to Singapore. And so *Renown* was made the flagship of this eastern fleet. We carried the admiral's flag and his staff, and I was on the admiral's staff as the fleet fighter direction officer.

"When I was appointed the Fleet fighter direction officer to the eastern fleet, which was just forming in England, I was the youngest lieutenant-commander in the Navy. I was 22 then, a new department really for the Navy but a vital one, as we controlled all the fighters both on the carriers and on the shore when we were within range of RAF bases."

On 15 December 1943 *Renown* hoisted the flag of Vice Admiral A. S. Power, Second in Command, Eastern Fleet (to Admiral Sir James Somerville).

"I had a fortnight earlier actually left *Renown* to go to *Formidable*, one of our big fleet carriers being refitted in

Belfast, but when Admiral Power arrived in *Renown* and no doubt conscious of the last admiral to take a fleet out to the Far East, Tom Philip who was sunk off Singapore in the *Prince of Wales*, he insisted that I returned to *Renown* to join his staff as Fleet direction officer. I was promoted to lieutenant-commander when just 23 years old and thus began an interesting last two years of the war for me."

Renown sailed shortly after Christmas for the East, in company with the battleship HMS *Queen Elizabeth*, the fleet carrier HMS *Illustrious* and escorts, and arrived at Trincomali on 27 January 1944.

"And so this fleet, the biggest fleet we had put together during the war, consisted of four battleships, with *Renown* as the flagship, and included a French battleship, and, of course, there were Polish destroyers and cruisers, French destroyers, Greek destroyers, all were in the same fleet, quite a multilingual fleet, and of, course, the Suez Canal was open then. We passed through the Suez Canal so there was no secrecy; the whole world knew that we were sending a fleet to the Far East, and we were based in Ceylon, a beautiful island."

These were busy months for Balme. In order to show the Americans that it could pull its weight in the war against Japan and cover the long distances involved, the Royal Navy had to learn the art of replenishment at sea, and the Fleet Air Arm also had much to learn from the US Navy, which had made rapid advances in naval aviation.

"Every few weeks the fleet or part of it would sail out across the Indian Ocean and bombard or bomb the old Dutch East Indies, [which were] now Japanese bases. At other times in harbour it was a life of constant practice and harbour exercises. It was my job to keep all the fighter direction and radar crews exercised with directing fighters against mock air attacks from the local naval air station. It was constant

> exercise month after month, only to be used in anger on about one occasion."

Operation Diplomat in March 1944 saw the Eastern Fleet, reinforced by the French battleship *Richelieu* and the Dutch cruiser HNLMS *Tromp*, practising refuelling at sea with the USN. In April, Operation Cockpit was an air strike by American and British carrier-borne aircraft on the oil tanks, shipping, aircraft and facilities at Sabang on the island of Pulau Weh at the northern tip of Sumatra. In mid-May the Eastern Fleet conducted Operation Transom, a strike by the Fleet Air Arm strike on Surabaya, Java, and it attacked Port Blair on 21 June. After a second air strike on 25 July on Sabang, the fleet closed the coast to bombard the town.

In August 1944 Admiral Sir Bruce Fraser took over from Somerville, when the Eastern Fleet was heavily reinforced, and the next operation was Millet, a prolonged series of air strikes and bombardment of the Nicobar Islands. In November command of the Eastern Fleet was split. Fraser became Commander-in-Chief, British Pacific Fleet, based in Sydney, taking with him much of the bulk of the former Eastern Fleet. Meanwhile, Power became Commander-in-Chief of the East Indies Station, based in Ceylon, and when, also in November, *Renown* was replaced as flagship by HMS *Queen Elizabeth*, Balme remained as Fleet fighter direction officer in the East Indies Fleet.

Balme summed up these operations:

> "And we used to go out and bombard the Dutch East Indies islands, which the Japanese had seized. We would bombard from about 15 miles away. Really just showed them we were there, we did a bit of damage but not much."

In the New Year of 1945 when a second wave of reinforcements arrived from Britain, an impressive force of escort carriers, the 21st Escort Carrier Squadron, was formed at Trincomali. Most of the ships belonged to the Ruler-class: *Ameer Begum*, *Emperor*, *Empress*, *Khedive*,

Shah, *Slinger* and *Speaker*: It was an historic moment when, in late February, Balme's admiral shifted his flag from the battleship *Queen Elizabeth* to the aircraft carrier *Empress* and she became flagship of the Eastern Fleet, for Operation Stacey. On 22 February *Empress* and *Ameer*, with the cruiser *Kenya*, destroyers and tankers now known as Force 62 (the British were beginning to adopt American terminology) sailed from Trincomali on 22 February for a series of reconnaissance missions in the eastern Indian Ocean. The dates 24–26 February found *Empress* off the Andaman Islands, where small groups of Japanese aircraft were seen on radar, but it was not until 1 March of that Balme directed a flight of four Grumman Hellcat fighters of 804 Naval Air Squadron from *Empress* to engage enemy aircraft, and one Japanese aircraft was shot down. Hellcats from *Ameer* claimed two more. These three aircraft were the first Japanese to be shot down by fighters flying from escort carriers.

Balme recalled this episode:

> "Between Sumatra and the Andaman islands, we were flying the flag in the small carrier *Empress* when at dawn the radar picked up enemy aircraft 60 miles away. Our fighter cover was already airborne and set out at once to intercept the enemy. I called up the admiral on the bridge and asked him to turn the fleet into wind so that I could order more fighters into the air. The whole thing worked like clockwork. The first flight of fighters were 20 miles out by the time we got the second flight airborne. Then at 30 miles from the fleet our fighters, who had been directed up sun and above the enemy, sighted the Jap air squadron. We took them by surprise and they were all shot down in a few minutes. And so months and months of practice had produced the result, which saved the fleet from even seeing an enemy aircraft."

Operation Stacey concluded with the fleet's aircraft carrying out a number of photographic sorties over the Kra Isthmus, Penang and the Similan Islands, and then over Sumatra and Sabang. By 6 March Force

62 had returned to Trincomali and air squadrons were flown off to their shore bases. The force entered harbour on 7 March. The effect of Operation Stacey may have been, in Balme's words "not much", but it was dramatic proof of principle in a new kind of warfare by the Royal Navy, and Balme was one of its pioneers. Force 62 had stayed at sea for fifteen days at some considerable distance from its base at Trincomali and Balme and his teams of direction officers and radio mechanics had shown how they could successfully direct fighters both from the battlecruiser *Renown* and from the escort carrier *Empress*.

Balme logged the following operations:

April 1944	Air strike Sabang
April	Air strike Surabaya
June	Bombardment Sabang
July	Air strike Port Blair
October	Bombardment Car Nicobar
January 1945	Arakan campaign
February	Photoreconnaissance of Kra Isthmus
March/April 1945	Bombardment of Sabang, air strike on Padang
3 May 1945	Assault on Rangoon
15 May 1945	Sinking of cruiser

The final phase of the war in the East was now approaching:

> "However the army were preparing to advance back through Burma and they would be supported by the Navy, and I was the staff officer on the admiral's staff who was sent up to Burma for a week to plan our invasion of the now Japanese-held Burma. It was very interesting, a very strange life, and I lived in a tent, and it was quite frightening in the dark. In the middle of the night, there'd be a rushing by the tent and a whole team of wild dogs would dash past. I found it very frightening, but I sealed up my tent and they never wanted to cut in, I'm glad to say."

The purpose of Balme's visit to the Army was to prepare for Operation Zipper, the British plan for landings on the Malayan coast prior to an advance on Singapore.

> "And so we planned, and then I had to get back to my ship. It was very difficult to get back, firstly the army would send me to Calcutta by car. I always remember arriving one night in Calcutta and the whole of the streets leading down to the big hotel which had been taken over by the British for officers and those in transit, and stepping over the bodies of Indians who were lying asleep in the road was a difficult job. You could tread on somebody's head. I just spent a night waiting for an aircraft and an aircraft took me down to Ceylon and I rejoined the flagship. We had very little opposition from the Japanese as we opened up our new front against them in Burma, so we weren't bombed in our ships, so we opened fire with our guns and drove the Japanese out of Burma, a difficult country with a lot of tropical diseases and animals.
>
> "We drove them out and gradually we captured all the great capitals, Rangoon, Singapore, etc. When we were down there, we were attacked by Japanese aircraft, and I had to organise, as Fleet fighter direction officer, the defence of the fleet. We used to pick up the enemy aircraft with our radar at about 70 miles range; we used to get our fighters in the air and they usually met the enemy aircraft about 40 miles out from the fleet. Which gave us plenty of space, but occasionally an enemy aircraft would get through and try and bomb the fleet. And then, of course, it was quite difficult because we wanted to open fire with our guns but our fighters were chasing enemy aircraft and we wanted to make sure that as they really got near us we called our fighters off, so they wouldn't be damaged by our own fire.
>
> "At any rate, this was all progress and we used to go in quite close to the shore, about 15 miles, and bombard various ports. And so we gradually pushed the Japanese back. I thought

it would go on for several years, but, of course, none of us knew about our secret weapon, the atom bomb. This saved so many lives that the USAAF dropping two of these enormous atom bombs on the Japanese big cities, and the Japanese surrendered within a week or two.

"And so we came to an end of the Far East war, which sometimes looked as if it might go on forever, over these enormous distances and the Japanese navy still quite strong with carriers.

"And so that seems to be just about the end of the war, the Japanese surrender which was a magnificent thing to hear."

The war and Balme's naval career were drawing rapidly to a close … .

19

HOME AGAIN

"And so I came back to England."

Balme was to receive one more appointment, to an admiral's staff at HMS Daedalus at Lee-on-Solent, where he first saw Susan, his wife-to-be. When she was sent to his office to get him to decipher his illegible handwriting, sixty-eight years of happy marriage followed.

WRNS Susan im Thurn while at Royal Naval Air Station, Burscough, 1945

An opportunity to leave the navy came in 1948, and Balme joined the family firm, a London wool broker, and this took him on frequent visits to develop the business in South Africa, Australia and New Zealand.

Balme the wool broker

In the mid-1950s Balme bought *Theme*, a small East coast smack, which was basic and intended to test Susan's tolerance for sailing small boats. *Theme* was soon upgraded to a beautiful Robert Clarke Clyde-built yacht, *Tanera*, and in the 1960s and 1970s Balme took up ocean racing. He bought Sir Maurice Laing's *Hephzibah* and competed in her for many years, when his navigation skills were exercised to great advantage. He was a long-standing member of the Royal Yacht Squadron, the Royal Ocean Racing Club and of the Royal Lymington Yacht Club. In the 1980s he retired to Lymington, where he continued to sail and to hunt with the New Forest Buckhounds.

David Balme out with the New Forest Buck Hounds

20

THE HOLLYWOOD YEARS

U-110 was not the only German – or Italian – submarine to be boarded or captured by the Allies during the Second World War, and among these the boarding of *U-570* in the Atlantic on 27 August 1941 is of relevance to David Balme's story.

The loss of so many U-boat aces in March 1941, including Günther Prien during the attack on Convoy OB293, Otto Kretschmer and Joachim Schepke during the attack on Convoy HX112, and, of course, of Fritz Julius Lemp in May, as well as the rapid wartime expansion of the U-boat fleet, had led to a noticeable thinning of experience among the officers and men of the U-boats. *U-570*'s untested and seasick crew had surrendered on their first patrol to an aircraft, and had been boarded from the trawler HMS *Kingston Agate*. A search had failed to find any cryptographic machine, and while *U-570*'s crew were taken prisoner on board the Canadian frigate HMCS *Niagara*, the U-boat was towed to Iceland, with an escort of circling Hudson and Catalina aircraft. There it arrived on 29 August and was beached in a sinking condition.

The interrogation of the crew of *U-570* revealed just how inexperienced they were: only the engineer officer and one or two petty officers had previously sailed on a war patrol, only one rating had more than 18 months' service, and "about half of the ratings, all very young, [had] joined the Navy in April, 1940, and the other half more recently than that date. Most of the technical ratings had done three to six months' U-boat training, the seamen even less."[83] However, the secret of the capture of *U-110* was already, only six months after the event, so completely hidden that the report of the interrogation of the prisoners from *U-570* clearly and plainly states that "*U-570* is the first U-boat to be captured in this war, her sighting and capture bringing great credit on the Navy and the Royal Air Force."

After three weeks she was salvaged, repaired and sailed for Britain under her own power, where she was commissioned as HMS *Graph* and made three operational patrols under the White Ensign. The German crew had smashed the Enigma machine and thrown the pieces overboard, but copies of encrypted signals and their corresponding, plain-language texts and the U-boat commander's handbook, which gave German naval procedures and abbreviations, were found and were to prove useful at Bletchley.

Meanwhile, Captain Daniel V. Gallery USN was attached to the staff of the US Naval Attaché in London in 1941, and in 1942 he took command of the USN air base at Reykjavík, Iceland. At some time, somehow, in London or later in Reykjavik, Gallery learned something of the Royal Navy's success in capturing *U-570*, and when in January 1944 he was promoted to rear-admiral and appointed to be commander of Task Group 21.12 with the escort carrier USS *Guadalcanal* as his flagship, Gallery conceived his own plan to emulate the British capture of *U-570*. On 4 June 1944 the hapless *U-505* duly became the first foreign man-of-war to be captured in battle on the high seas by the US Navy since the War of 1812. However, when Gallery published a book about this in 1957 – which ran into many editions – he started a different war, a war of words.[84]

So well had the secret of the boarding of *U-110* kept that when Captain Stephen Roskill wrote four volumes of *The War at Sea*, published in the years 1954 to 1961, no one told him of it, and the first edition of the first volume of Roskill's history in 1954 blandly recorded that *U-110* was sunk.[85] This was not part of any deception: when he wrote his history Roskill did not know other than that *U-110* had been boarded and ransacked. Soon however, Baker-Cresswell and others hinted at the truth to Roskill, and Baker-Cresswell told him that he was seeking permission to write an account of events, and he had seventy-odd pages dealing with the secret capture of a German U-boat.

Now when Roskill read Gallery's account of his capture of *U-505* he became incensed. In his words:

> "Certain of the claims which he [Gallery] made for his own ship and service would not hold water, and the whole matter of the capture of enemy submarines between 1939 and 1945 had got badly out of perspective ... and it is a fact that well before Admiral Gallery towed *U-505* triumphantly into Bermuda we had boarded and searched several others – and had said very little about it ... the capture of *U-110* in 1941 far transcended in importance the capture of *U-505* by Admiral Gallery and his men just three years later."

Roskill, whose intellectual spat with an American historian, Arthur Marder, was brewing, saw an opportunity to score a point. Pausing briefly from his magnum opus, the official history of the war at sea, Roskill sought permission to write about the capture of *U-110*, a permission which he was given "under the same conditions as imposed on a Baker-Cresswell's proposal" and within a few months in 1959 Roskill dashed off a book that he called *The Secret Capture.*[86] Evidently one of those conditions was that Roskill would not reveal the secret of the pinch of Enigma and for the careful reader there are just a few clues, for those already in-the-know about *U-110*, that the significance of the secret capture was not the U-boat herself but her contents. There is a reference, for example, to "books, logs, charts and moveable equipment" being taken on board *Bulldog*.

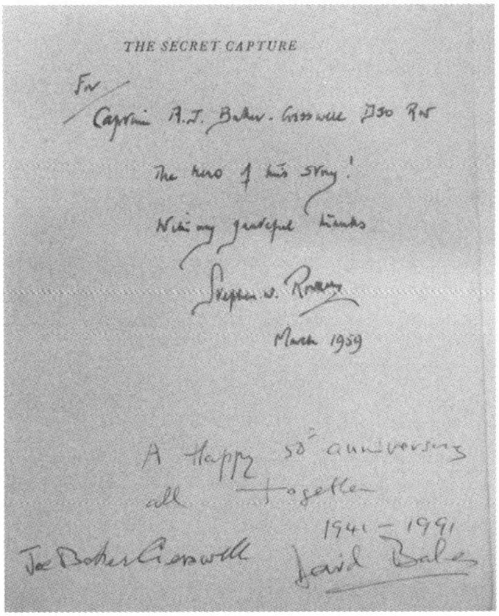

Title page of The Secret Capture, signed by Roskill, Baker-Cresswell, and Balme (Baker-Cresswell)

Apart from this brief war of words across the Atlantic, for fifty years the boarding of *U-110* remained almost forgotten, and Roskill's book did little to publicise the affair. All the British participants in Operation Primrose felt bound by the oath of secrecy to which they had been sworn in 1941. When the wider secret of Enigma was revealed – some would say betrayed – by F. W. Winterbotham in 1974, attention turned to the significance for the historical record of prior knowledge through signals intelligence of German and Italian plans, how this affected the analysis of the war, and a revision of the history that had been written to date.[87] One of those who revised the history of war was David Kahn, whose book, *Seizing the Enigma: The Race to Break the German U-Boat Codes, 1939–1943*, published in 1991, is one of the best accounts of this secret war.[88] Meanwhile, even those closely involved in the secret capture did not know the full nature of the pinch: Barry Sheen, who had been first lieutenant of HMS *Aubretia*, the ship whose attack had brought *U-110* to the surface and who became a High Court judge, wrote in 1988: 'I did not know that you took the cipher machine out of *U-110* until I read Patrick Beesly's *Very Special Intelligence*.'[89]

In 1998, a documentary called *The Secret Capture of U-110* was based on Kahn's book and made for American television. The documentary finishes by saying that 'the three greatest naval actions of the last 200 years are Trafalgar, Midway and the capture of *U-110*, which was so brilliantly conducted by Captain Baker-Cresswell, from HMS *Bulldog*, after an accurate depth charge attack by HMS *Aubretia*.' Inspired by this, Jonathan Mostow wrote a movie called *U-571*. The movie *U-571* transferred the filming to the Mediterranean and the heroes became Americans. When it became known that Universal Studios had cast a bunch of Americans as the heroes who captured Enigma, in a mirror of the spat that had prompted Roskill to write his book, an outcry was raised in Britain, an outcry that even reached the House of Commons.

David Balme's name was first heard in the House of Commons when his MP, Julian Lewis, mentioned him in 1998:

> "I want to pay tribute to someone whom I regard as representative of the generation that did so much to ensure our freedoms, a constituent of mine, David Balme. As a Sub-Lieutenant aged 20 on HMS *Bulldog*, when it had trapped the German U-boat *U-110* – which could have blown up or sunk at any second – he led a boarding party onto the submarine and seized from it the Enigma codes, precipitating one of the turning points in the intelligence battle of the Atlantic. While yesterday we were remembering those who did not survive the tremendous battles, it is appropriate to pay tribute, in the context of a Royal Navy debate, to people like David Balme, and the young men who fought with him and survived, who by heroic measures – he was awarded the Distinguished Service Cross – helped keep the sea lanes open and win the Battle of the Atlantic, and helped us to survive as a free and democratic country."

The following year MPs condemned Universal's plans to rewrite history, while Julian Lewis, more thoughtfully noted that while "the US film industry is willing to take far greater poetic licence ... I wonder whether, even at this late stage, representations might be made to the American producers to allow a walk-on part to my constituent, the then Royal Navy sub lieutenant David Balme DSC, who actually captured the Enigma machine from the *U-110* seven months before America even entered the war?"

The result of Lewis's intervention was that Balme was co-opted into the filmmaking by Jonathan Mostow, who was now the movie's director as well as screenwriter. Mostow recalled:

> "The outcry in the U.K. began shortly after we began filming in Rome – well over 16 months before the film's release in theaters. I was disheartened because the British newspapers had grabbed onto the story without benefit of any of the facts: no journalist knew the film's plot or had read the screenplay, much less had bothered to interview myself, the producers or

anyone from Universal Pictures. The story took on a life of its own and soon-after, politicians began piling onto the melee of bad publicity.

"As someone who had uniformed family members wounded or killed while battling German forces in Europe and North Africa, I was particularly troubled by the accusation that we were causing an affront to the memory of British sailors who had served valiantly in the Battle of the Atlantic. If we were indeed making a travesty of history, I decided no one was better equipped to make that determination than the British officer who had personally seized the enigma from a German U-boat and hence, was presumably the greatest victim of this historical controversy.

"I obtained David Balme's contact information (I believe from historian David Kahn, who I had befriended during the course of my research), and I simply phoned and introduced myself. David had heard of the controversy by this point and so he was initially skeptical, but he was also open to learning more and was understandably curious to see what all the fuss was about. By that point in the production, we had moved to Malta, so I invited David to come and witness the filming for himself.

"David arrived in Malta with his wife Susan and I gave them carte blanche to speak with everyone and ask any questions they cared to. And then after the film was edited, I invited David to Los Angeles to view it and give his opinion. I knew I was putting myself and the film at great risk because if he objected, it would mean that our critics were right – and we would face a public relations disaster. But I was also confident that our best spokesman was the film itself – and that in my heart, I knew we were not guilty of the accusations that had been leveled at us over the preceding year.

"We were pleased that David embraced the film, but alas, media stories like these are hard to unwind once established, so while I am personally gratified to have received David's approval, I accept that there will always be those in England who view the film negatively."

Balme himself was:

> "A bit surprised and initially I thought it was a pity. But I don't know why anyone complains because no one had heard of this before the Americans made the film, and it brings home the whole Battle of the Atlantic to a generation who otherwise would have known nothing about it. Once I got working with them I realised that the scale they were going for was beyond the budget of a British film."

Balme spent two weeks in the company of the crew during filming in Malta and he bonded with the film's stars, Matthew McConaughey, Jon Bon Jovi and Harvey Keitel. "They were a marvellous bunch. Matthew McConaughey is a terribly nice chap. Harvey Keitel has a wonderful manner and is a fantastic actor." Balme's sentiment was reciprocated and Mostow wrote that he was "humbled and honored if

David and Sue Balme with the stars of the movie U-571: left to right, Bill Paxton, Jon Bon Jovi, (David and Susan), Matthew McConaughey (Balme)

I was able to play even a tiny role in helping to bring added attention to David's extraordinary achievements. The service that he so bravely performed on May 9 of 1941 was arguably the single most important action that turned the Battle of the Atlantic, and by extension, possibly the entire war. Getting to personally know David ranks as one of the great privileges of my life."[90]

Some thought was given to a walk-on part as a coastguard for Balme, but he settled in a role of historical advisor. However, Balme failed to convince Mostow to open the movie with a message that it was a work of fiction. The film was a hit, a huge success in the US and number four in the UK box office chart on its opening weekend in March 2000, but it was again condemned in the House of Commons for its rewriting of history as an affront to British sailors. It noted:

> "[That British sailors] risked their lives to board the stricken submarine, facing the danger that it might sink at any time. That members of the boarding party were decorated for their heroism in retrieving the encoding device and that King George VI described their actions as perhaps the most important single event in the war at sea. And regrets that Hollywood has chosen to distort the truth and detract from the valour of the British sailors concerned by appropriating the story for its own financial gain."

Balme on the casing of 'U-571' in Malta in 1999 (Balme)

However, Julian Lewis's intervention and David Balme's participation in the filmmaking did win an important concession at the end of the movie, before the credits rolled: a dedication honouring the Royal Navy's role in the capture of *U-110*. Balme wrote about this:

> "I thought you would like a report on my time in Hollywood. After all the press criticisms in March of the film stealing a British action, I have been helping them and watched the filming in Malta and now I have seen the finished film called *U-571*. It is really an excellent and gripping film set in the Atlantic with good credits to the British.
>
> "The director and author of *U-571*, Jonathan Mostow, has been inundated with requests for recognition of various actions in the Battle of the Atlantic. In the end he decided, and I think very wisely, to include just three credits covering the only three times when U-boats were ever actually boarded: (1) *U-110* in May 1941, quoting HMS *Bulldog*, HMS *Aubretia* and the 3rd Escort Group. No German survivors saw us boarding, so security was 100%, (2) *U-559* in October 1942 quoting HMS *Petard*. This is when 2 men lost their lives and were awarded the GC, which somewhat impaired the security, (3) *U-505* in June 1944 by the US Navy and towed to Bermuda, but as the German survivors knew she had been boarded, security was again jeopardised. *U-505* is now on show in Chicago.
>
> "These credits give a pleasant Anglo-American flavour just as the bipartisan approach to it all in Parliament. The credits are shown with the American survivors of the battle paddling their life raft ashore with the sun setting behind them. Audiences will see these credits as they are part of the film and not muddled up with that long list of actors, directors etc."

There was one side effect. Balme had been haunted by memories of the fear he had felt while climbing down inside *U-110* sixty years before. The boat could have been sinking, booby-trapped or had charges set to scuttle her, or someone could have been waiting below to take their

David and Sue Balme in Malta inspect the faux U-570's gun (Balme)

revenge by shooting him. "Going down those ladders and thinking there may be Germans ready to shoot you ... it was terrifying. We couldn't believe that they would have just abandoned this submarine. It was something that haunted me for 15 or 20 years afterwards." The making of *U-571* had reawakened these nightmares.

Nevertheless, Balme remained positive about Hollywood's interpretation of events, and by the time that Prime Minister Tony Blair was agreeing in a brief exchange in the House of Commons that the movie was an affront to the memory of British sailors, Balme had already seen *U-571* twice and he thoroughly approved:

"It's a great film. It's all blood and thunder and the young people will love it."

21

CODA

Balme was not the only officer ever to have boarded a German U-boat. The little corvette HMS *Arbutus*, commanded by Temporary Lieutenant Arthur Warren, RNR, already had her share with HMS *Camellia* in the sinking of *U-70* on 7 March 1941. Having hunted *U-70* for five hours, when the U-boat was blown to the surface *Arbutus* prepared to ram, but stopped when the Germans were seen to be jumping overboard, and *U-70*, though still under way, seemed to be sinking rapidly by the stern. *Arbutus* just missed *U-70* and, as she glided by, she dropped two Carley floats near the survivors and, turning, picked up twenty-six Germans, including the U-boat's commander. Perhaps it was thinking upon this experience that helped to make *Arbutus* ready when two months later, on 4–5 April 1941, with the destroyers *Wolverine* and the sloop *Scarborough*, *Arbutus* hunted *U-76* through the night and in mid-morning blew her to the surface. Once more the interrogation report commented on the "marked lack of experience" of her crew, but they seemed to have made an orderly evacuation of their boat, whose batteries were almost exhausted and which had been shaken by a number of depth charge attacks. As *U-76* wallowed in the Atlantic rollers, the little *Arbutus* signalled for the second time in her short career that she was about to ram a U-boat, and once more she hauled off when the U-boat's crew were seen to be abandoning ship.

This time however, *Arbutus* nuzzled alongside the stricken German and her first lieutenant, Temporary Lieutenant Geoffrey

Barrett Angus, RNVR and three seamen jumped on to the German boat's casing. They did not know that the Enigma machine had been smashed to pieces prior to *U-76*'s surfacing, and Angus made an attempt to enter the boat. The boat remained afloat for at least half an hour while *Arbutus* attempted to pass lines around her to prevent her sinking. However, when Angus peered down the conning tower hatch, the control room was clearly flooded and there was the whiff of chlorine gas coming up from the batteries. Angus slammed the hatch and dogged it tightly, but it was almost too late and to save *Arbutus* from being pulled over by the weight of the German U-boat and from a possible capsize, the ship let go of her capture. All but one member of the crew survived and these were picked up by *Wolverine*. It was a brave attempt to capture a German U-boat and to Angus must go the honour of being the first British officer to board a U-boat at sea.[91] He was awarded the DSC, and his sailors were mentioned in despatches or awarded the DSM.

Later in the Second World War another significant boarding of a German U-boat took place, this time in the Mediterranean. The German *U-559* was off Alexandria when she was detected and hunted by the destroyers HMS *Dulverton*, *Hurworth*, *Pakenham* and *Petard*. On the evening of 30 October 1942, after repeated depth-charging, a badly damaged *U-559*, with a cracked pressure hull, unable to maintain level trim, with four dead already from explosions and flooding, and her batteries nearly exhausted, was forced to surface. *Petard*, commanded by Lieutenant Commander Mark Weston, illuminated her by searchlight and opened fire with her guns.

As the crew abandoned ship, the U-boat was boarded by three men from *Petard*: Lieutenant Tony Fasson, Able Seaman Colin Grazier and teenage NAAFI canteen assistant Tommy Brown. All three climbed down into the flooded boat and successfully removed the Enigma machine, with its current settings, and other cipher material from the sinking boat. However, the boat was settling in the water and despite shouted warnings from Brown, Fasson and Grazier were drowned as the U-boat sank and water flooded down the conning tower. They were awarded the George Cross and the youthful Brown was awarded the George Medal. Apparently consideration was given to awarding Fasson and Grazier the Victoria Cross but this was denied them as, technically, their bravery was not performed in the face of the enemy.

The awards to the officers of men of HMS *Arbutus* in April 1941 and of HMS *Petard* in October 1942 contrast slightly oddly with the awards to the men of the 3rd Escort Group in May 1941. Balme's bravery may not have been directly in the face of the enemy, but he could not have known for certain that *U-110* was deserted, and his bravery was not shown in the red mist of anger that, for example, enables a man to charge a machine gun post against all odds, nor was it for accomplishing a set numbers of dangerous missions, say flying on bombing raids over enemy territory.

Rather, Balme had had several minutes while he coxed *Bulldog*'s whaler over the Atlantic swell towards the U-boat, not knowing whether there might be someone at the top of the conning tower waiting to shoot him, to contemplate the danger to himself and to his boat's crew. He had boarded the U-boat over her wet, slippery sides with all the risks of sliding into the sea, and he had then climbed down inside the boat into the face of danger. It was, he said, "a very nasty moment 'cos both my hands were occupied with the rungs of the ladder going down so I didn't have a revolver and I was a sitting target to anyone down below." The dangers were that someone was waiting for him at the bottom of the ladder as he descended feet first into the unknown, that the boat might be filled with poisonous chlorine gas leaking from the batteries, that scuttling charges might blow up at any instant, or that the boat was already flooding and might sink at any moment.

At the bottom of the ladder he was met by almost complete and eerie silence: this itself must have been unnerving for there is always a hum of background noise in every ship or submarine. Instead he was greeted by "a most unpleasant and frightening noise" except for an ominous hissing sound that he knew must come either from compressed air leaking out of its reservoirs or water from water leaking into the hull, and the lighting gave a dim, ghostly effect. Despite this alien environment, Balme then searched the boat from end to end to ensure that there was nobody left on board, conscious all the time that as the boat rocked in the Atlantic swell she was also listing to port. Only when he was satisfied that there was no one else on board did he call some of the rest of his boarding party down. Then, when *Bulldog* disappeared into the mist – visibility at best had only been a few miles – he listened to the sound of depth charges around him while EG3 hunted for other U-boats, all the time fearing that the shock might set off any charges in the boat, and unsure whether – in the days before satellite navigation – the *U-110* would be found again. When a submarine sinks (rather than deliberately submerges) it loses buoyancy until the sea pours over the conning tower and down the hatch, to entomb anyone inside: that was the ultimate danger that faced Balme.

Balme's pinch saved countless Allied ships and lives, brought about the end of numerous U-boats and their crews, and shortened the Second World War. Historians are unanimous in placing the highest rank on the event. Ronald Lewin, for example, wrote that, 'History is written in terms of Trafalgars and Jutlands, but by any standards the seizure of *U-110* should be rated as a major victory at sea.'[92] John Winton assessed the importance of the pinch as ultimately leading two years later to a German retreat from the North Atlantic, which was a strategic victory as important as the Battle of Midway in the Pacific and the Battle of Stalingrad in Europe.[93] The American historian David Kahn concluded his television documentary by saying that 'the three greatest naval actions of the last 200 years are Trafalgar, Midway and the capture of *U-110*, which was so brilliantly conducted by Captain Baker-Cresswell, from HMS *Bulldog*, after an accurate depth charge attack by HMS *Aubretia*.'

Undoubtedly the hunt for *U-110* was a team effort by the ships and men of the 3rd Escort Group led by Commander Joe Baker-Cresswell. The Enigma machine had been initially found by Alan Long, and the ransacking of the interior of *U-110* had been conducted by several men from HMS *Bulldog*, including Lieutenant Commander George Dodds. However, the supreme bravery, knowing and conscious of the dangers, in first venturing on to and into the

U-boat was Balme's and for this he was given the Distinguished Service Cross. The citation read:

> "For smartness and efficiency in boarding and salving books and documents of great value. It should be recognised that this officer knew of the danger of booby traps and from the likelihood of the operation of a demolition charge. While in the submarine depth charges were detonating at no great distance. There was therefore the possibility of attack by torpedo from another U-boat, despite these dangers, the task of salving important documents was carried out thoroughly and carefully."

At his investiture on 17 February 1942, King George VI told Balme: "This should be a much higher award, but the Germans would wonder why, and it will be put right at the end of the war."

Balme, who died on 3 January 2016 aged 95, never succeeded in calling in this Royal promise.

Ned and Jack Balme hold their great-grandfather's medals (Balme)

APPENDIX A – ABSTRACT OF THE SIGNALS LOG

Signals are rare survivors in the archives: they are ephemerae and signal logs were routinely destroyed a short time after they became time-expired. However, in 2016 an exceptional hoard of signals about the boarding of *U-110* was found in at The National Archives at Kew. See: TNA ADM 237/33 Admiralty: Naval Staff: Operations Division: Convoy Records, Second World War OB318. Someone, perhaps aware of the historic significance of the capture of *U-110*, has tipped the signals higgledy-piggledy into the two parts of this file. Arranged chronologically they also tell the story of the capture, boarding and the sinking of *U-110* in the terse prose of 'signalese'.

Extract from the signals in ADM 237/33 OB 318 parts I and II

Time of origin	Date	From	To	Extract
1625	05/051941	CINCWA	Bulldog etc.	Sail EG3 in time to meet OB318 … at 1800Z 7th May …
1704B	07/05/1941	Admiralty	EG7	Enemy submarine has made a first sighting report of a convoy or important unit probably OB318 or escort joining at 1357Z … alter course to starboard
1223Z	08/05/1941	*Bulldog*	CINCWA	U/boat was almost certainly stopped on convoy track
1332Z	08/05/1941	*Bulldog*	CINCWA	*Bulldog* and *Amazon* re-joining OB318. Contact died away at 0045Z after 9 attacks by *Bulldog, Amazon* and *Rochester*

1935B	08/05/1941	CINCWA	*Ranpura* etc.	Escorts will be required to leave in time to RV with HX124 ... on 12th May
2107B	08/05/1941	Admiralty	*Bulldog etc.*	Enemy submarine has made a first sighting report at 1822Z/8 of a convoy or important unit
1145B	09/05/1941	CINCWA	*Bulldog etc.*	OB318 disperse at daylight May 10th escorts remain in loose company during May 10th
1252B	09/05/1941	Admiralty	*Bulldog etc.*	Enemy submarine has made a first sighting report at 0950 Z/9 of a convoy or important unit probably OB318 ... Alter course to port
?	09/05/1941	EG3	*Aubretia*	This is your bird
1859Z	09/05/1941	EG3	CINCWA	4 ships sunk. Attacked by 2 or 3 U-boats. One of which possibly sunk. German s/m U-110 [in] tow of *Bulldog* at 6 knots. Important books and gear recovered. 4 German officers and 26 men in *Aubretia*. 3rd Escort Group has practically no depth charges
2050Z	09/05/1941	*Bulldog*	CINCWA	*Broadway* [damaged?] in forward fuel tank. She has 80 tons left and is escorting *Bulldog* to Iceland
0430B	10/05/1941	CINCWA	*Bulldog*	Your 1859Z Splendid
0830	10/05/1941	Admiralty	CINCWA, *Bulldog etc.*	Capture of U-110 is to be referred to as operation Primrose. Operation Primrose is to be treated with greatest secrecy and as few people allowed to know as possible
	10/05/1941	CINCWA	All staff officers	*Bulldog's* achievements is to be considered MOST SECRET and all departments are to warn their staff not to mention it to anyone
0842B	10/05/1941	Admiralty	EG3	... Give names of HM ships which know Primrose was not sunk and do not permit them to enter harbour without further orders

1044Z	10/05/1941	EG3	Admiralty	Reference Primrose consider souvenirs so vital they should reach home without [delay?]. Nothing (?) destroyed. Should welcome discussion with CINCWA
1110Z	10/05/1941	EG3	Admiralty, CINCWA, FO Iceland	Afraid weather has cheated … Primrose has sunk. Have been hove to in rising sea since 0700 ... German officers and men now in *Amazon* ... Consider petals of primrose of utmost importance
1735	10/05/1941	Flag Officer, Iceland	*Amazon*	Confirm that all prisoners are on board *Amazon*. Their presence is to be regarded as secret and ship's company it to be warned accordingly
1938	10/05/1941	*Admiralty*	CINCWA	Primrose having sunk makes it no less important that fact of having had her in our hands should remain secret. This fact is to be rigorously impressed on all who have knowledge of facts
1922	11/05/1941	Flag Officer, Iceland	Admiralty	Ship companies … have been warned
1221Z	12/05/1941	EG3	CINCWA	From interrogation of prisoners Primrose followed in Broadway's wake at 10 knots ... Captain Lemp who was lost (considered second only to Prien) expected we should have left convoy …
1802B	12/05/1941	*Bulldog*	Admiralty etc.	*Bulldog* arrived at Scapa
2310B	13/05/1941	First Sea Lord	*Bulldog*	Hearty congratulations. The petals of your flower are of rare beauty
1441B	28/06/1941	Admiralty	*Bulldog*, *Broadway*, *Aubretia*	Their Lordships congratulate you your officers and ships company upon the destruction of a German U-boat on 9 May 1941

NOTES:

1. CINCWA is, the Commander-in-Chief Western Approaches, Admiral Sir Percy Noble.
2. The zone time: Z is Greenwich meantime, which was in use in the Atlantic, and B is GMT, +2 hours i.e. double British summertime, which was used in wartime Britain.
3. The signal at 2310B/13 from the First Sea Lord, Admiral Sir Dudley Pound, is not at Kew but in the Baker-Cresswell archives in the Northumberland Archives, Woodhorn.

APPENDIX B – THE TIMETABLE OF OPERATION PRIMROSE

The logs of the ships of the 3rd Escort Group, which hunted and captured *U-110* on 9 May 1941, have not survived, but it is possible to recreate a timetable of the day from the ship's reports of action against submarines, and the various reports of proceedings in the archives at Kew. The fullest account with timings comes from HMS *Aubretia* and other timings within EG3 are in agreement. Where timings are not known, the sequence of other events has been inferred from their order in various narratives.

Time	Event
1200	*Aubretia* Lat 60° 31’ N Long 33° 10’ W. Wind WSW 4. C.6. Sea 3 Swell 2. Visibility 5 miles. *Aubretia* was stationed on the starboard beam of the convoy, zig-zagging independently. Convoy steering 220°
1201	*Aubretia* steering 190 at 10 knots and distant 800 from No 9 Column, abeam of No 92. Ships No 91 and 41 were torpedoed. Speed increased to 13 knots and course altered to starboard intending to drop one charge. The torpedoes were heard by the S.D. on watch and a report was made by R/T that the attack was from the starboard side.
1202	Two ships, *Esmond* and *Bengore Head*, torpedoed.
1203	*Aubretia* obtains contact bearing 335° dist. 1000 [yards] but was not held probably due to ship being under helm. Aubretia was steadied in 340° and engines stopped in order to regain contact.

1204	*Aubretia* sights periscope bearing 000° travelling from port to starboard, distant 800 (approx). Course was altered to 030° at full speed and a counter-attack carried out.
1204½	*Aubretia* obtains faint trace.
1206	*Aubretia* attack no I completed.
1208	*Broadway* attacks.
1210½	*Aubretia* stops engines to listen.
-	*Bulldog* and *Broadway* join hunt.
1215	*Aubretia* obtains contact.
1220	*Aubretia* attacks.
1223	Attack no II completed.
-	*Aubretia* attack puts ASDIC out of action.
-	*Aubretia* hauls off to allow *Bulldog* and *Broadway* to hunt.
1235	*Bulldog* sights a conning tower at about 800 yards range on the port beam.
1239	*Aubretia* rescues *Esmond*'s survivors.
-	*Bulldog* and *Broadway* in gun action with surfaced U-boat.
-	*Bulldog* orders *Aubretia* to pick-up U-boat survivors.
-	34 German prisoners taken from water by *Aubretia*. 2 die on board
1245	Balme leaves *Bulldog* in ship's whaler.
-	*Bulldog*'s whaler washed onto *U-110*'s casing and smashed
-	*Bulldog* orders *Broadway* to close and lower a boat.
-	First ERA from *Bulldog* arrives in *U-110*.
-	Engineer Officer, Gunner (T) and second ERA arrive in *U-110*.
-	Bulldog passes first tow to U-boat.
1322	*Aubretia* ASDIC set repaired.
	[1426 *U-201* sinks *Gregalia* and badly damages *Empire Cloud*.]
1430	*Broadway* obtains contact while screening *Bulldog*.
1432	*Bulldog* sights periscope. Towed slipped.
1432	*Aubretia* joins *Broadway* in hunt for a U-boat:

[1435	*Broadway* attacks underwater contact.
1437	*Aubretia* obtains contact.

1441	*Aubretia* attacks.
1443	*Aubretia* attack no III completed.
1452	*Broadway* attacks.
1500	*Aubretia* and *Broadway* in contact with underwater target.
1516	*Broadway* obtains marked hydrophone effect.
1519	*Aubretia* in contact.
1520	*Aubretia* attacks.
1523½	*Aubretia* attack no IV completed.
1532	*Broadway* attacks.
1535	*Broadway* obtains contact.
1536	*Broadway* attacks.
1538	*Broadway* attacking.
1545	*Aubretia* in contact, listening.
1550	*Aubretia*'s contact faded.]

1550+	*Aubretia* ordered to search round *Bulldog*.
1600	*Broadway* ordered to screen *Bulldog*.
-	*Broadway*'s boat makes two journeys to bring back books, charts and documents.
1600	Baker-Cresswell orders men in *U-110*: "Batten down and prepare to take on tow".
1600+	*Bulldog* passes second tow to U-boat.
	[*c.* 1730 Hunt for *U-201* by *Amazon*, *Nigella* and *St Apollo* ends after dropping ninety-nine depth charges, which cause severe damage, but *U-201* escapes on surface during the night.]
-	*Aubretia* screens *Bulldog* until ordered to close *Amazon* and transfer prisoners.
1830	All back in *Bulldog*.

10/1100	*U-110* sinks.
11/0100	*Bulldog* arrives Hvalfjord.
11/0630	*Amazon* hands over U-boat prisoners.
12/1830	*Bulldog* arrives Scapa Flow.
13/0830	Prisoners leave *Bulldog*.
13/1530	Two wounded prisoners leave *Bulldog*.

BIBLIOGRAPHY

Baker Cresswell, Joe, Letter, 1981, Baker Cresswell to Balme, Balme private papers.

Balme, David Edward, Balme, David Edward (London: IWM 12023, 1991).

Battle of the Atlantic (BBC London: Andrew Williams, 2002).

Beesly, Patrick, intro W. J. R. Gardner, and afterword Ralph Erskine, *Very Special Intelligence: The Story of the Admiralty's Operational Intelligence Centre 1939–1945*, 2nd edn (London: Greenhill Books, 2000).

Blair, Clay, *Hitler's U-Boat War: The Hunter, 1939–1942* (New York: Modern Library, 2000).

Brown, David, *The Royal Navy and the Mediterranean Vol II: November 1940–December 1941* (London: Frank Cass Publishers, 2002).

Daily Telegraph, 'How Sea Enigma Fell Into British Hands', 1988.

Daily Telegraph, 'U-Boat Captured Without A Shot', 1988.

Dimbleby, Jonathan, *The Battle of the Atlantic: How the Allies Won the War* (London: Penguin, 2015).

Divine, A. D., *The Merchant Navy Fights: Tramps against U-Boats* (London: John Murray, 1940).

Dodds, George, "Commander (E) George Edwards Dodds", Commandergeorgedodds.org, 2016, http://commandergeorgedodds.org/Commander_George_Dodds/Photos.html#7 [accessed 27 January 2016].

Dodds, Malcolm, *Life and Times of Commander (E) George Edward Dodds* (Risborough: Privately published, 2010).

Dönitz, Karl and R. H. Stevens, Memoirs: *Ten Years And Twenty Days* (London: Weidenfeld & Nicolson, 1958).

Erskine, Ralph, 'Naval Enigma: A Missing Link', *International Journal of Intelligence and Counterintelligence*, 3 (1989), 493–07.

Erskine, Ralph, 'Naval Enigma: The Breaking of Heimisch and Triton', *Intelligence and Natural Security*, 3 (1988), 162–83.

Gallery, Daniel V., *We Captured A U-Boat* (London: Sidgwick and Jackson, 1957).

Green, Jimmy, 'BBC – WW2 People's War – Capture of the Enigma Machine', bbc.co.uk, 2016, www.bbc.co.uk/history/ww2peopleswar/stories/77/a3672777.shtml [accessed 27 January 2016].

Hinsley, F. H, E. E. Thomas, C. F. G. Ranson, and R. C. Knight, *British Intelligence in the Second World War: Its Influence on Strategy and Operations Vol I* (London: HMSO, 1979).

Hinsley, F. H, E. E. Thomas, C. F. G. Ranson, and R. C. Knight, *British Intelligence in the Second World War: Its Influence on Strategy and Operations Vol II* (London: HMSO, 1981).

'HMS Renown, British Battlecruiser, WW2', Naval-history.net, 2016 www.naval-history.net/xGM-Chrono-02BC-Renown.htm [accessed 20 January 2016].

Kahn, David, *Seizing the Enigma: The Race to Break the German U-boat Codes, 1939–1943*, 2nd edn (Barnsley: Frontline, 2012).

Lavery, Brian, *Churchill Goes To War: Winston's Wartime Journeys* (London: Conway, 2007).

Lewin, Ronald, *Ultra Goes to War* (New York: McGraw–Hill, 1978).

Paterson, Lawrence, *The First U-Boat Flotilla* (Barnsley: Leo Cooper, 2002).

Pollock, William Stewart (London: IWM 11948, 1991).

Price, Alfred, 'The Desert Hornet's Nest', *Flying Review International*. 20 (1964).

Roskill, Stephen Wentworth, *The Secret Capture* (London: Collins, 1959) since republished in 2011 with a new foreword by Charles Baker-Cresswell and introduction by Professor Barry Gough.

Roskill, Stephen Wentworth, *The War at Sea, 1939–1945 Vol I* (London: H.M. Stationery Office, 1954).

Sebag-Montefiore, Hugh, *Enigma: The Battle for the Code* (London: Weidenfeld & Nicolson, 2000).

Seymour, A. M., Letter, 1991, Balme private archives.

Shanhan, Phil, *The Real Enigma Heroes* (Stroud: The History Press, 2010).

Sheen, Sir Barry, 'Secret Legacy of Captured U-Boat', *The Times*, 1997.

Showell, Jak P. Mallmann, *Enigma U-Boats: Breaking the Code – The True Story* (Shepperton: I. Allan, 2000).

Smith, Vivian Funge, Letter, 1957, Balme private papers.

Stewart, Ninian, *The Royal Navy and the Palestine Patrol* (London: F. Cass, 2002).

The Times, 'Obituaries: Captain A. J. Baker Cresswell', 1997.

The Times, 'Obituaries: Commander Allon Bacon OBE RNVR', 1990.

'U-Boat Archive – U-110 – Interrogation Report CB 4051 (23)', Uboatarchive.net, 2016, www.uboatarchive.net/U-110A/U-110INT.htm [accessed 19 January 2016].

'U-Boat Archive – U-570 – Interrogation Report', Uboatarchive.net, 2016, www.uboatarchive.net/U-570/U-570INT.htm [accessed 31 January 2016].

Winterbotham, Frederick W., *The Ultra Secret* (London: Weidenfeld and Nicolson, 1974).

Winton, John, *Ultra at Sea* (London: Leo Cooper, 1988).

NOTES

1. David Balme's memoirs, his letters and extracts from his midshipman's journal are set in quotation marks, and any short explanatory notes by the editor are set within in square brackets. In addition to recordings in the Balme family archive, David also recorded his memoirs for the Imperial War Museum: see Balme, David Edward, *Balme, David Edward* (London: IWM 12023, 1991). The editor is also grateful to Julian Lewis for his loan of a recording of a talk which David gave to the Lymington Conservative Association.

2. Stewart, Ninian, *The Royal Navy and the Palestine Patrol* (London: F. Cass, 2002), pp 13–15.

3. Blair, Clay, *Hitler's U-Boat War: The Hunter, 1939–1942* (New York: Modern Library, 2000), pp 110–15.

4. Divine, A. D., *The Merchant Navy Fights: Tramps against U-Boats* (London: John Murray, 1940).

5. Brown, David, *The Royal Navy and the Mediterranean Vol II: November 1940–December 1941* (London: Frank Cass Publishers, 2002), pp 3–28.

6. TNA ADM 358/3065 HMS Berwick: 27 November 1940: damaged by enemy action. 25 December 1940: damaged by enemy action in the North Atlantic.

7. TNA ADM 53/111569 HMS *Berwick* Ship's Log for December 1940.

8. Notes entered in Lemp's pocket diary, captured on 9 May 1941, show *U-30*'s first war patrol began on 22 August 1939, twelve days before the outbreak of war. Lemp reached his war station on 29 August, and five days later, on Sunday, 3 September, Lemp duly noted that England and France had declared war on Germany. Apparently nothing occurred during the following week that Lemp thought worthy of notice, for there is no further entry in his calendar until 10 September.

9. Northumberland Archive, Woodhorn (NAW) ZBC box 19 item 4. 'Flimsy' dated 13 March 1941 and covering the dates 27 July 1939 to 21 November 1940.

10. NAW ZBC box 20 item 4. Undated and unsigned but in the hand of A. J. Baker-Cresswell *The Capture of U110 or the Best Kept Secret of the War*, this 76-page manuscript is a first draft of the book that eventually emerged under S.W. Roskill's name as *The Secret Capture* (1959). A copy is in Roskill's papers at Churchill College Archives ROSK 7/6 part 2/2.

11. NAW ZBC box 20 item 4, p 46.

12. The zone times of various reports is not given and appears to be inconsistent.

13. Blair, Clay, *Hitler's U-Boat War: The Hunter, 1939–1942* (New York: Modern Library, 2000), pp 278–95.

14. EG3, although so far west was keeping Z time or GMT, so meridian passage would not be until 14:09 (and sunset not until 22:33).

15. TNA ADM 217/33 part II.

16. Baker Cresswell, Joe, letter dated 26 December 1988, Balme private papers.

17. Baker Cresswell, Joe, letter dated 28 May 1991, Balme private papers. See also TNA ADM 137/4156 Signal code book (Signalbuch der Kaiserlichen Marine (SKM) copy no 151) captured from cruiser *Magdeburg*, August 1914 by Russians and handed to Room 40, October 1914.

18. Baker Cresswell, Joe, letter dated 15 February 1988, Balme private papers.

19. Ibid.

20. Ibid.

21. NAW box 20, Balme letter to S. W. C. Roskill, 5 May 1958.

22. NAW box 20 item 4, p 44.

23. Pollock, William Stewart (London: IWM 11948, 1991). Pollock's presence in the party to board *U-110* is confirmed by (1) Balme in IWM 12023, 1991, (2) Seymour, A, M,, letter dated 10 December 1991 to Balme, Balme private papers: "Captain Baker Cresswell told me of the error in not including Pollock in the honours list and he had been unable to get it corrected later" and (3) Baker Cresswell letter dated 2 June 1981 to Balme, Balme private papers: "the unfortunate Pollock whose name was omitted from the list of the boarding party."

24. See also Funge Smith, Vivian, letter dated 23 December 1957 on board SS British Skill to Captain S. W. Roskill, Balme private papers.

25. NAW ZBC box 20 item 4, p 46.

26. Baker Cresswell, Joe, letter dated 2 June 1981 to Balme, Balme private papers.

27. Smith, 1957.

28. Sheen, The Hon Justice Mr Barry, letter dated 15 February 1988 from the Royal Courts of Justice, Balme private papers.

29. Sheen, Sir Barry, 'Secret Legacy of Captured U-Boat', *The Times*, 15 March 1997.

30. Dimbleby p 202. Unfortunately the interviewer did not ask why the Enigma machine and the code material had not been destroyed or dumped overboard.

31. NAW XBC box 19 item 19.

32. Uboatarchive.net, 'U-Boat Archive – U-110 – Interrogation Report CB 4051 (23)', 2016, www.uboatarchive.net/U-110A/U-110INT.htm [accessed 19 January 2016].

33. Costello, John and Terry Hughes, *The Battle of the Atlantic* (London: Collins, 1977).

34. Paterson, Lawrence, *The First U-Boat Flotilla* (Barnsley: Leo Cooper, 2002), p 82. The false allegation was also quite disgracefully repeated, in a different form, in *The Times*, 'Obituaries: Captain A. J. Baker-Cresswell', 6 March 1997.

35. *Battle of the Atlantic* (BBC London: Andrew Williams, 2002).

36. Dimbleby, Jonathan, *The Battle of the Atlantic: How the Allies Won the War* (London: Penguin, 2015) pp 201–03.

37. Beesly, Patrick, intro WJR Gardner, and afterword Ralph Erskine, *Very Special Intelligence: The Story of the Admiralty's Operational Intelligence Centre 1939-1945*, 2nd edn (London: Greenhill Books, 2000).

38. Winton, John, *Ultra At Sea* (London: Leo Cooper, 1988).

39. Kahn, David, *Seizing The Enigma: The Race To Break The German U-Boat Codes, 1939–1943*, 2nd edn (Barnsley: Frontline, 2012).

40. Sebag-Montefiore, Hugh, *Enigma: The Battle for the Code* (London: Weidenfeld & Nicolson, 2000).

41. *Daily Telegraph*, 'U-Boat Captured Without A Shot;, 11 February 1988; *Daily Telegraph*, 'How Sea Enigma Fell Into British Hands', 29 January 1988; this false accusation first surfaced in 1977 in a book by a British author – that it has been repeated with seemingly graphical detail in an otherwise generally reliable work of reference (Paterson, Lawrence, *The First U-Boat Flotilla* (Barnsley: Leo Cooper, 2002), p 82) does not make it any less untruthful.

42. NAW ZBC box 20 item 7. Balme to S. W. Roskill 5 May 1958.

43. Pollock, William Stewart (London: IWM 11948, 1991).

44. Dodds, Malcolm, Life and Times of Commander (E) George Edward Dodds (Risborough: Privately published, 2010), pp 9–10. See also ZBC box 20 item 7. Balme: "I shall never forget the sight of the Chief stuck in a watertight door. He was going from one compartment to another and there was a nasty swell on. The door must have swung to onto him and I am afraid, while it was very painful to him, it was extremely funny to see the look on his face, with depth charges all around while he was stuck in the doorway."

45. Dodds, George, 'Commander (E) George Edwards Dodds', *Commandergeorgedodds.org*, 2016, http://commandergeorgedodds.org/Commander_George_Dodds/Photos.html#7 [accessed 27 January 2016].

46. Green, Jimmy, 'BBC – WW2 People's War – Capture of the Enigma Machine', *bbc.co.uk*, 2016, www.bbc.co.uk/history/ww2peopleswar/stories/77/a3672777.shtml [accessed 27 January 2016].

47. www.telegraph.co.uk/news/obituaries/2437896/Commander-Alec-Dennis.html

48. Confidential Admiralty Fleet Order (CAFO) 1544 – German Cyphering Machines (NID 02688/40 – 29.8.1940). The editor is grateful to W. R. 'Jock' Gardner for finding this reference.

49. Hinsley, F. H., E. E. Thomas, C. F. G. Ranson, and R. C. Knight, *British Intelligence in the Second World War: Its Influence on Strategy and Operations Vol I* (London: HMSO, 1979), pp 336–39.

50. Erskine, Ralph, 'Naval Enigma: A Missing Link', *International Journal of Intelligence and Counterintelligence*, 3 (1989), pp 493–507.

51. Hinsley, F. H., E. E Thomas, C. F. G. Ranson, and R. C. Knight, *British Intelligence in the Second World War: Its Influence on Strategy and Operations Vol II* (London: HMSO, 1981), p 163.

52. Winton, John, *Ultra at Sea* (London: Leo Cooper, 1988), p 146.

53. TNA ADM 186/806 Interrogation of German naval survivors, CB 4041(23). See also www.uboatarchive.net/U-110A/U-110INT.htm.

54. Groves.

55. The Times, 'Obituaries: Commander Allon Bacon OBE RNVR', 20 October 1990.

56. Beesly, Patrick, intro W. J. R. Gardner, and after Ralph Erskine, *Very Special Intelligence: The Story of the Admiralty's Operational Intelligence Centre 1939–1945* (London: Greenhill Books, 2000), p 71.

57. Sebag-Montefiore, Hugh, *Enigma: The Battle for the Code* (London: Weidenfeld & Nicolson, 2000), p 141.

58. Roskill, Stephen Wentworth, *The War at Sea, 1939–1945 Vol I* (London: H.M. Stationery Office, 1954), pp 463, 466.

59. Beesly, p 72.

60. TNA ADM 1/11133 Convoys and Escorts: U-boat attacks on Convoy OB318 and counter attacks by HM Ships resulting in capture of U-boat *U-110*.

61. TNA ADM 199/658 Western Approaches Command: War Diaries, 1941.

62. TNA ADM 199/2058 Monthly anti-submarine reports Vol 2, 1941.

63. TNA ADM 186/806 CB 04051(23) *U-110* Interrogation of Survivors.

64. Hinsley, *Vol II*, pp 164–5.

65. Hinsley, *Vol I*, pp 345–46.

66. Dönitz, Karl, and R. H Stevens, *Memoirs: Ten Years And Twenty Days* (London: Weidenfeld & Nicolson, 1958), pp 143–45.

67. Richard Woodman, *Malta Convoys 1940–1943* (John Murray, London, 2000), pp 329–39.

68. The hotel was totally destroyed in anti-British riots on 26 January 1952, part of the 'Cairo Fire' that led to the 23 July Revolution. A modern hotel called the Shepheard Hotel was built nearby in 1957.

69. For further research the editor is grateful to Barbara Gilbert and Captain John de Winton at the Fleet Air Arm Museum and to Commander David Hobbs.

70. Price, Alfred, 'The Desert Hornet's Nest', *Flying Review International*, 20 (1964).

71. The German surrender in North Africa took place on 12 May 1943.

72. Roskill, Stephen Wentworth, *The War at Sea, 1939–1945 Vol I* (London: H.M. Stationery Office, 1954), p 311.

73. Admiral of the Fleet Sir Alfred Dudley Pickman Rogers Pound (1877–1943) and First Sea Lord (1939–43). Pound's illnesses prevented him from sleeping at night and he used to doze off at meetings. After a stroke he resigned in September 1943, and died of a brain tumour on Trafalgar Day.

74. General Hastings Lionel 'Pug' Ismay (1887–1965), Indian Army officer who became Churchill's chief military assistant during the Second World War, later also the first Secretary General of NATO (1952–57)

75. Éamon de Valera (1882–1975) Irish leader in the struggle for independence from the United Kingdom and in the Irish Civil War (1922–23) who served several terms as head of government/head of state including Taoiseach (1937–48) during the Second World War. Founding member of the Fianna Fáil party.

76. Brendan Bracken (1901–58), 'Churchill's Irishman', an Irish businessman, newspaperman, MP and Minister of Information 1941–45. He eschewed popularity and limelight and though elevated to the peerage never used his title nor sat in the House of Lords.

77. *Claudia* (1943), a romantic comedy starring Dorothy McGuire, Robert Young, Ina Claire, etc.

78. *Wintertime* (1943), a musical romance starring Sonja Henie, Jack Oakie, Cesar Romero, etc.

79. Presumably *Holy Matrimony* (1943), a wartime comedy starring Monty Woolley, Gracie Fields, and Laird Cregar: Fields made three films in 1943.

80. *Eternal Father, Strong to Save*: written in 1860 by the English hymnist William Whiting (1825–78) and inspired by Psalm 107, is associated with seafarers, particularly of the USN and RN, the last verse *For those in peril on the sea/O Trinity of love and power/ Our brethren shield in danger's hour/From rock and tempest, fire and foe/Protect them wheresoe'er they go/Thus evermore shall rise to Thee/Glad hymns of praise from land and sea* used to be sung while kneeling at Dartmouth.

81. Wing Commander Sir John William Maxwell 'Max' Aitken, DSO DFC (1910–85).

82. Lavery, Brian, *Churchill Goes to War: Winston's Wartime Journeys* (London: Conway, 2007); see also Naval-history.net, 'HMS Renown, British Battlecruiser, WW2', 2016, www.naval-history.net/xGM-Chrono-02BC-Renown.htm [accessed 20 January 2016].

83. Uboatarchive.net, 'U-Boat Archive – U-570 – Interrogation Report, 2016, www.uboatarchive.net/U-570/U-570INT.htm [accessed 31 January 2016]. The secret of the capture of *U-110* was already, six months later, so completely buried that this report clearly and plainly states that, "U-570 is the first U-Boat to be captured in this war and her sighting, capture and bring great credit on the Navy and the Royal Air Force."

84. Gallery, Daniel V, *We Captured A U-Boat* (London: Sidgwick and Jackson, 1957) Roskill would have been even more incensed had he known that Gallery's book would become a bestseller, rarely out of print and translated into several languages.

85. Roskill, Stephen Wentworth, *The War at Sea, 1939–1945 Vol I* (London: H.M. Stationery Office, 1954), p 463.

86. Roskill, Stephen Wentworth, *The Secret Capture* (London: Collins, 1959). Since republished in 2011 with a new foreword by Charles Baker Cresswell and introduction by Professor Barry Gough. The book was written so hastily that Roskill omitted the important pinch from the Italian submarine *Durbo* made on 18 October 1940 east of Gibraltar that enabled the sinking of a second Italian boat, *Lafolè*, two days later. For the record, 20-year old Sub Lieutenant Peter Meryon, Petty Officer Harold Brown and Stoker Petty Officer George Andrews were the first Britons in the Second World War to board and make a pinch from an enemy submarine.

87. Winterbotham, Frederick W, *The Ultra Secret* (London: Weidenfeld and Nicolson, 1974).

88. Kahn, David, *Seizing The Enigma: The Race to Break the German U-Boat Codes, 1939–1943* (Boston: Houghton Mifflin Co., 1991). Revised and republished in 2011 by Frontline, Barnsley.

89. Sheen, The Hon Justice Mr Barry, letter dated 15 February 1988 from the Royal Courts of Justice, Balme private papers.

90. Email to the editor from Jonathan Mostow, 15 March 2016, 19:34.

91. Blair, Clay, *Hitler's U-Boat War: The Hunter, 1939-1942* (New York: Modern Library, 2000), pp 265–66.

92. Lewin, Ronald, *Ultra Goes to War* (New York: McGraw–Hill, 1978)

93. Winton, John, *Ultra at Sea* (London: Leo Cooper, 1988), p 146.

INDEX

numbers prefixed with 'f' refer to the list of numbered footnotes commencing on page 156

3rd Cruiser Squadron 20
3rd Destroyer Flotilla 7–14
3rd Escort Group ix, 30, 33, 38–9, 139, 143–4, 147–50
3rd Minesweeping Squadron 3
5th Escort Group 35
7th Escort Group 39–40
8th Army 100, 103
21st Escort Carrier Squadron 124
811 Naval Air Squadron 8
822 Naval Air Squadron 8
826 Naval Air Squadron 99, 102–3
    pioneers in path-finding 103–4

Aitken, Max 121
Alamein, El 102–5
Albacore, Fairey 93, 98, 103, 107
Alexander, General 119
Alexandria 2, 19–21, 81, 93, 96, 98–100, 103–6, 120–1, 142
Algiers 107
Amazon, HMS 39–40, 53, 63, 70, 82–3, 85, 88, 146, 148, 152
Ameer, HMS 124–5
Andaman Islands 125
Angle, HMS 40
Angus, Lt Geoffrey Barrett 141–3
Anson term, Dartmouth 2
Antelope, HMS 94
Arabistan, SS 24
Arbroath 93
Arbutus, HMS 141–2
Arcadia, meeting 113
Argus, HMS 20, 23–4, 94
Ark Royal, HMS 19–20,
Arrow, HMS 38
Athenia, SS 33-4, 52, 84
Atlantic, Battle of ix
Aubretia, HMS 39–40, 42–53, 66, 70, 81–3, 134, 139, 144, 147–8, 150
Bacon, Lt Allon 85–6
Baden, German blockade-runner 25
Badoglio, Italian Marshal 113
Baker-Cresswell, Captain Joe ix, 30, 36–49, 53, 62, 65–71, 82, 85–9, 132–4, 149, f10, f16–20, f23, f26, f34
Baker-Cresswell, John 36–7,
Balme, Charles, ancestor 1
Balme, David
    crash-lands 105
    hunting 130
    Ivanhoe, HMS 1
    midshipman 1
    origins in France 1
    rescued by HMS *Rye*, 96
    sailing 130
    sand-fly fever 106
Balme, François, ancestor 1
Balme, Jack, father 2
Balme, John, brother 16
Balme, Susan, wife x, 129–30, 136
Barham, HMS 19,
B-Dienst 11
BdU, German U-boat command 9, 36, 39, 75, 91
Bedouin, HMS 95
Beesly, Patrick 54–5, 87, 134
Benghazi 105
Bengore Head, SS 42, 150
Bermuda 36, 133, 139
Berwick, HMS 17
    [illegible] ships 17
Bild am Sonntag 54
    retracts allegation of murder 54
Birkenhead 18, 38
Birmingham, HMS 70
Bismarck, German battleship 89, 113
Bletchley Park vii, x, 76, 78–9, 85–6, 132
Bon Jovi, Jon 137
Bonaventure, HMS 23–5
Bracken, Brendan 117–8, f76
Bretagne, French steamer 13

British Pacific Fleet 124
Broadway, HMS 39–40, 42–5, 49–50, 53, 59, 61, 63, 66, 68-70, 84, 147–8, 151–2
Broom, Marine Denis 25
Brown, NAAFI Assistant Tommy 142–3
Bulldog, HMS 26–46, 47–55, 56–87, 88–91, 92, 133–9, 143–4
hunts for *U-110* 150–2
signals to/from 146–8
sister ships 27
Burdwan, SS 94–5

Cairo, Egypt 68, 96–8, 100, 112, 120–1, f68
Cairo, HMS 94
Calcutta 127
Camellia, HMS 141
Canada 27, 31, 33, 38, 82, 84, 113, 116, 131
Carr, Able Seaman Robert W 5, 57
Catalina, flying boat 131
Channel Islands 29
Channel, the English 11
Chant, US merchant ship 93–6
crew desert Balme 95
Charybdis, HMS 94
Chiang Kai-shek 120
China 33, 113
Chissell, Stoker Henry 21
Chocolate, Operation 100–1
Churchill, Mary 115
Churchill, Mrs 117–8
Churchill, Sir Winston x, 112–22
'Winston special' 22
'Claudia', film 119
Clyde, Firth of, river, etc. 19, 23, 30, 38, 76, 113, 130
Cockpit, Operaton 124
Collar, Operation 20
Collingsworth, US freighter 9
Continental, hotel in Cairo 97
Convoy HX112, 35, 131
Convoy KJF3 x, 11–14, 75
Convoy OB260 25
Convoy OB293 35, 131
Convoy OB318 x, 33–45, 54, 146, f60
signal log 146–149
Convoy SC31, 89,
Convoy WS5A 21–6
convoy escort 23
Copeland, Barry 51
Costello & Hughes, journalists 53
Courageous, HMS x, 7–9
Cunningham, Admiral 'ABC' 19, 21

Daedalus, HMS 129
Daily Telegraph 54, f41
Daneman, HMS 39–40
Dau, Rolf 11
Davison, Cpl Robert 25
Dearing, Susan x
Dekheila *see* HMS *Grebe*
Denmark 16
Denmark Strait 22, 89
Dido, SS 9
Dimbleby, Jonathan 54
Diplomat, Operation 124
Dodds, LtCdr George ix, 59–71, 144, f44–45
Dodds, Malcolm x, 60, f44
Dolley, Able Seaman Cyril 67
Dönitz, Konteradmiral Karl *see* BdU
Dulverton, HMS 142
Dutch East Indies 123–4

Eagle, HMS 94
Eastern Star, SS 40
Ecke, Helmut, war correspondent 36, 47, 52–3, 83
prisoner no 2 81
Egypt 2, 23, 100, 103, 105, 120
Eichelborn, Hans Joachim 34, 47, 53, 78, 82
Empire Cloud, SS, 63
Empire Trooper, SS 23–4
Empress, HMS 124–6
Erodona, SS 35
Esmond, SS 42, 50, 52, 70, 150–1

FAA 20, 92, 109, 123–4
Fasson, Lt Anthony 142–3
Fields, Gracie 119, f79
Fighter Direction x, 107, 109-13, 120, 122
Finland 16
Fleet Air Arm *see* FAA
Force F 19–20
Force H 19
Fork, Operation 18
occupation of Iceland 18
France 1, 16, 35, 25, 30, 38, 75, 81, 84, 121, f8
Fraser, Adm Sir Bruce 124
Frost, PO Cook Leslie 21
Furious, HMS 23–4

Gallery, Adm Daniel, USN 132–3, f84
Gardner, Jock x, f37, f48, f56
GCCS *see* Bletchley Park
Gelhaar, Alexander 13
Genoa 113

George V, HM the King 2, 138
  the King's promise 145
Germany 9–10, 16, 18, 21-6, 29, 38
  war declared on 6, 84, f8
Gibraltar 19–21, 25–6, 93–4, 120–1
  local flotilla 30
Glasgow 33, 112
Gonzenheim, German supply ship 89, 113
Graph, HMS ex *U-570* 132
Grazier, Able Seaman Colin 142–3
Grebe. HMS 96, 99, 103
Greece, Athens, etc. 20, 29, 37
Green, Jimmy 71, f46
Greenland 31, 39, 42
Gregalia, SS 63
Groves, Lt 85
Guadalcanal, USS 132

Haifa 4–5
Halifax 31, 35, 113, 117
Hamilton, RAdm Louis 86
Hargreaves, Ordinary Seaman Arnold 67
Harpoon, Operation x, 92–7
Hartmann, Werner 11–14, 75
Hayter, Gunner John 12
Hearst press 118
Hebrides 36
Hellcat, Grumman fighter 125
Henie, Sonya 119, f78
Henri Mory, SS 36
Hephzibah, yacht 130
Higgs, Lt Walter 45, 67
Hipper, German cruiser x, 22–5
Hobbs, David x, f69
Hodgkinson, Cdr George 2
Högel, Georg 35, prisoner no 1 81
Hollyhock, HMS 39–40
Hollywood 118
Hood, HMS 89
Howard, Leslie 110
Hudson, Lockheed 102, 131
  Balme flies to Cairo 96
Hulley, LSBA Cyril 21
Hurworth, HMS 142
Hvalford 39, 53, 152

Icarus, HMS 12–13
Iceland 35, 38–9, 41, 53, 66, 68–70, 85, 89, 91, 131–2, 147
  flag officer 148
Ilex, HMS 11–12
Illustrious, HMS 19, 123
Imogen, HMS 11–12
Implusive, HMS 6, 9
Inglefield, HMS 9
İnönü, Mustafa İsmet 121
Ismay, General 117, 119, f74
Italy, Italian fleet, etc. 93, 100, 134
  air force 94
  cruisers 20, 95–6
  submarine 131, f86
  surrender 113, 117
  targets 102
Ivanhoe, HMS 1, 4–7, 9–10, 12–14, 57, 75

Japan x, 20, 122–28
Jewish refugees 3–5, 33
Jones, Cdr Basil 5
Jones, Prof RV vii
Judgement, Operation 19
Jumna, SS 25

Kafiristan, SS 8
Kahn, David vii, 54, 134–6, 144, f39, f88
Karamea, SS 13
Keitel, Harvey 137
Kentucky, US merchant ship 93
Kenya, HMS 94, 125
Kerneval 38
Kingston Agate, HMS 131
Kra Isthmus 125
Kretschmer, Otto 35, 131
Kuppisch, Herbert 39–40

Lee, Stoker Cyril 67
Lemp, Fritz-Julius 33–6, 40–4, 47–55, 62–5, 71, 77, 82, 84, 131, f8
  return of Iron Cross 53
  state of mind 41, 88
  suicide 53, 56
Lewin, Ronald 144
Lewis MP, Dr Julian x, 134–39, f1
Libya 100
Lightfoot, Able Seaman John 21
Lisbon 110
Liverpool 23, 35, 39, 49, 94
Liverpool, HMS 94
Lochavon, SS 13
Loewe, Dietrich 34, 47, 49
London Gazette 12, 90
London, HMS 2
Long, Telegraphist Alan 67, 74, 90, 144
Lützow, German cruiser 89
Lyons, Marine Reginald 25

MacIlwain, AB James 21,
Macintyre, Cdr Donald 35
Mackenzie, RAdm WB 36
Magdeburg, Germen cruiser vii, 45, f157
Malaya 127
Malaya, HMS 94
Malta 20, 93–6, 106–7, 120
filming in 136–40
Marder, Arthur 133
Marines *see* Royal Marines
Masterman, Sir John vii
Mathews, ERA 83–4
McConaughey, Matthew 137
Mediterranean 2, 6, 18–20, 30, 79, 95, 98, 109, 112–14, 142
convoys, fleet 7, 20, 96, 113
Mersa Matruh 100
Miller, Lt 97
Millet, Operation 124
Morgan-Giles MP, RAdm Morgan 103
Mostow, Jonathan x, 134–9, f90
Mountbatten, Adm Lord Louis 30, 113
'Mountbatten pink' 38

Nabarro, Joan viii
Naiad, HMS 21
Neptune, HMS 113
Neptune, Operation 113
New Forest Buckhounds 130
New Zealand 37, 130
Newfoundland 112
Newsday, New York x
Niagara, HMCS 131
Nicobar Islands 124
Nigella, HMS 39–40, 152
Noble, Adm Sir Percy 37, 149
Norway 16–8, 76

O'Brien, Cook James 81–2
Orari, SS 94–5
Otrato, freighter 3
Overlord, Operation 113

Painter, Sgt Charles 25
Pakenham, HMS 142
Palestine, Patrol x, 3–6, f2
lessons of 57
Partridge, HMS 95
Pearce, Able Seaman Sidney 67
Pearl Harbour 20
Penang 125
Perlas, schooner *Las* 4–5, 57
Petard, HMS 139
'pinch'
from the Germans ix, 76–8, 80, 84–5, 88–9, 133–4, 144, 161
from the Italians f86
from *U-110* 78–80
Pollock, Wireless Telegraphist William 49–50, 56–9, 64, 67, 70–1, 90, f23, f43
Port Blair 126
Pound, Adm of Fleet Sir Dudley 86, 117, f73
Power, Adm Sir Arthur 122–3
Prien, Günther 35, 131, 148
Primrose, Operation 66, 69–70, 86, 88, 90, 134, 147–8, 150
Pulau Weh 124

Quadrant, meeting 113
Queen Elizabeth, HMS 123–5
Queen Mary, RMS 113

RAF 98
absent, 95
copies Op Chocolate 101–2
out of range 100
Ramillies, HMS 20–1
Rangoon 126–7
Ranpura, HMS armed merchant ship 39, 147
Renown, HMS 20, 112–22
Resolution, HMS 30
Reykjavik 18, 39, 68, 85–6, 88, 132
Richelieu, French battleship 124
Rochester, HMS 40, 146
Roe, Able Seaman Richard 67
Ropner, Sir R 11–12
Roskill, Capt S W ix, 48, 50, 53, 132–4, f10, f24, f42, f58, f84–6
Royal Lymington Yacht Club 130
Royal Marines 18, 25, 100, 115
Royal Ocean Racing Club 130
Royal Yacht Squadron 71, 130
Russia 16
Rutledge, Able Seaman William 42
Rye, HMS 96

Sabang 124–6
Sardinia 18, 94
Saumarez, LtCdr Philip 11–12
Scapa Flow 18, 30, 53, 70, 79, 85, 89, 113, 148, 152
Scarborough, HMS 141–2
Schepke, Joachim 35, 131
Schnee, Adalbert 41, 53, 63
Schnurzl, fox terrier 35

Sebag-Montifiore, Hugh 54, f40, f57
Sextant, conference 120
Sheen, Lt (later Hon Justice) Barry 51, 134, f28, f89
Shepeard's, hotel in Cairo 98
Shipman, Steward John 12
Shropshire, HMS 2
Sidi Barrani 99
Similan Islands 125
Singapore 122, 126–7
Skua, dive-bomber 24
Smith, Captain Albert 11–12
Smith, LtCdr Vivian Funge 39, 42, 50, f24
Sollum 100
Somerville, VAdm James 19–20, 122–4
Spain, inc. Spanish Civil War x, 2, 22, 29, 94
Spartivento, Battle of Cape x, 17–21, 112
St Apollo, HMS 39–40, 152
Stacey, Operation 125–6
Stalin, Josef 121
Stevens, Cdr EBK 11–12
Stewart, Ninian x, f2
Stonepool, SS 11–13
Styles, CPO Cook James 21
Suez Canal 100
Sumatra 124
Supply ships, German, destruction of, 89
    Gedania 89
    Gonzenheim 89
Surabaya 124–6
Sutton, HMS 2
Sweden 16
Swordfish TSR 8, 19, 24–5, 94, 98, 99–103
Sydney 124

Talbot, Captain Arthur 11
Tamaroa, SS 23
Tanera, yacht 130
Tanimbar, Dutch merchant ship 94
Taranto, Battle of 19–20
Taylor, Lt Cdr Thomas 39, 44–5
Tedder, AVM Sir Arthur 102
    praises role of FAA 107
Theme, East Coast smack 130
Tobruk 81, 100–1
Tovey, Adm Sir Jack 85–6
Transom, Operation 124
Trincomali, Ceylon 123–7
Tripoli 105–7
Troilus, SS 94
Tromp, Dutch cruiser 124
Trotter, Ordinary Seaman John 67

U-29 9
U-42 3–13
U-45 13
U-47 35
U-53 8
U-70 141–2
U-76 141–2
U-94 36, 39
U-99 35
U-100 35
U-110 36, 131–9, 143–7, 150–2, f32
    loot from *U-110* 63–64
U-505 132–3, 139
U-559 139, 142
U-570 131
U-571, a fictional U-boat 134, 137–40
Universal Studios 134–6
USA 38
    not in the war 38
    USAAF drops atom bombs 128
    USN 39, 124, 132

Valera, de 118
Vanoc, HMS 35
Veendam, Dutch liner 9
Vigorous, Operation 93, 96

Walker, HMS 35
Warren, Lt Arthur 141
Wehrhöfer, Ulrich 34
    prisoner no 3 82
Welshman, HMS 94
West, Wolfpack 33
Western Approaches 7–8, 11, 37–8, 71, 86, 88, 149, f60
Western Desert x, 93, 96, 98–107
Weston, LtCdr Mark 142
Wilde, Heinz 52
Wildman, SurgLt William 21
Wileman, Able Seaman Claude 67
Willis, RAdm A 37
Winant, John Gilbert 120
Winter Time', film 119, f78
Winter War 16
Winterbotham, Frederick vii, 134, f87
Winton, Captain John de x, f69
Winton, John (author) 54, 144
Wolverine, HMS 141–2
Woodman, Richard x, f67
WRNS 70, 113, 115, 17

Zipper, Operation 127